WHAT NOBODY KNEW

Amelia Hendrey

ISBN 978-1-912145-72-0

@iamselfpub
www.iamselfpublishing.com

This is the story of my life. I wanted to show you my story because I am living proof that when life seems like it is set on giving you a really rough time, the only mode you should set your body to is survival mode. Everyone has a story to tell, but I am a survivor, and I will show you why. Hopefully, if you can relate to anything in the book, it can give you strength to know that you can come out the other side. In some of the book, there are snapshots of my memories because that is all I can remember at that time. Throughout the whole book are documents that explain the other half of my story – the parts I wasn't witness to, don't remember or wasn't aware of. In the official documents through this book, I have protected the identity of all adults by referring to them as either Mr or Mrs.

CONTENTS

PART ONE: *EARLY MEMORIES*

PART TWO: *SCHOOL AND TEENAGE MEMORIES*

PART 3: *LIFE AFTER SCHOOL*

PART ONE

EARLY MEMORIES

CHAPTER ONE
My First Memory

Age 3

They say you don't retain your memories until you're five. This is a memory I have when I was three: my mother left me.

It was a Saturday afternoon; the town centre was its normal bustling self with people everywhere. I remember the sound of the market stall men roaring with their big voices, 'Come and get it, a pound a bowl,' along with the chatter of people going about their day-to-day business.

I held my mother's hand tightly because all the people made me nervous. Her soft hand in mine made me feel safe. We came to a clearing and she crouched down to me. I looked up at her, squinting as the sun hit my face from behind her head.

'Stay here,' she said softly. 'I need to go to that shop and I'll be back in a minute.' And with that, she left.

There are other accounts of what happened.

People say she left me on my nan's doorstep at 10p.m., rang the doorbell then ran away.

I have no memory of that.

But that's not to say it didn't happen.

Chapter Two
Barbara

Age 4

Dad met Barbara while she was picking up glasses outside the pub where she worked. Barbara soon came into our lives to stay.

She was a very large lady – as wide as she was tall – and had always been that size (she had told me this herself). Because of her large build, in her younger days, she had been asked to play in the boy's rugby team, which she declined.

She told me once that she was constantly bullied at school for her size, and having long hair didn't help her. Her hair was so long that she could tuck it right under her bum when she sat down. She said she found this out because if she left her hair hanging over the back of the chair in class, the boys would tie it around the chair, and when the teacher would ask her to stand, she would get up and scream in pain. In turn, the teacher would give her the cane for screaming, and then she would then go home and tell her mum, who would give her the cane for getting the cane.

Maybe that's why she kept her hair in a short bob as an adult.

She smoked like a chimney, just like Dad, but unlike him, she wasn't a drinker. She constantly reeked of self-pity. She liked to read and get lost in a book with all its wondrous tales and facts. She was a loner, desperate to be loved, and I think when Dad came along, she jumped at the opportunity and grabbed it with both hands.

She had been married before and had other children. They were grown up and had families of their own, but they very rarely saw her. She always blamed Dad for them not coming around.

I was five the first time he hit her. She should have run for her life at that point, but she didn't. Instead, she would hype up the stories of him hitting her and overdramatise it. I'm not saying that him hitting her wasn't bad, because it definitely was. It was just her, who she was. She used to overdramatise everything; it gave her a story to tell people. Maybe for the first time in her life, she was being seen, being noticed and not hiding in the shadows. It wasn't a good life but it's one people saw. She would happily tell the neighbours and show off her bruises.

We were like two strangers who lived in the same house, shared the same experiences, but one was in charge. I was never close to her; I don't know why we never connected. She was more like a glorified babysitter than a parent and she always saw me as a burden. She wasn't the lovey-dovey type that wanted to hang out, cuddle, have in-depth talks, or play in the garden. She was very selfish and preferred gossiping with the neighbours than talking with me. If I went outside to sit on the step while she was talking across the fence to them, she would bark at me, 'Go inside. Stop being so nosey.' Then she would let out a huge sigh and say to them, 'I never get any privacy, and she is not even mine. I chose to look after her.'

She was a manic-depressive. The doctor gave her pills for this, so her mood was either really high or really low. Each day, you didn't know if she was going to be overly positive or severely negative. A lot of the time, she was negative. Regardless of her mood, she would get up, make food and sit in the garden if it was nice weather or sit in her chair and watch TV. That was most days for her.

Because of her size, she couldn't walk that far, so we would either walk to the corner shop or taxi into town. On her overly positive days, she would get a surge of energy and walk at a faster pace than normal to the corner shop and back. The next day, her body would tell her she had done too much, and she would sit for a couple of days or stay in bed.

Normally, when we walked to the shop, she would have to stop a dozen times or more on the way there and back to have a breather, leaning up against lampposts, signs, bus stops, or even sitting on benches – just pit stops to get there and back. The weight pushing down on her heels and the effects of smoking were the two main reasons she felt the strain of walking. She didn't stop smoking, and she never lost weight, so she was in a Catch-22.

Sometimes, to show she was in charge when she was really depressed, she would hit me with her moccasin slipper. She would flail her arms around shouting, hating the world, then she would whack me with it all over my body. She would scream it was all my fault – 'it' being whatever was bothering her at the time. I would jump constantly as the moccasin hit hard. The leather would strike my skin and whip and burn the area, followed by a long-lasting sting.

When she was done, she would throw down the slipper and sit on the floor and cry. She didn't cry for long though; she would feel sorry for herself for a little bit then act as though nothing had happened. Sort of like a toddler's mini tantrum.

She would get up, take herself into the kitchen, make a cup a tea, and then head to the garden. Ten minutes or so later, I would hear her laughing with the neighbours. I'd look down and see that I was covered with red shoe imprints that stung like hell. Red balls of anger that hurt too much to touch.

I think a lot of the time, she struck out of frustration with Dad. She couldn't hit him so she hit me instead, or maybe it was just because she just hated her life.

CHAPTER THREE
Her Nose

Age 5

I was five the first time I remember the violence.

It was a Sunday. The pubs always shut earlier on a Sunday, so Dad always doubled up his drinks so that he could be drunk by the time it closed. I was sitting on the sofa when he fell through the front door, landing abruptly on the floor, where he lay laughing.

He got up and staggered towards me, swaying heavily left and right. He leant down to me, and he grabbed my nose in between the knuckles of his two fingers and said, '*Honk, honk.*' Then, he patted my face hard and said, 'I love you, mini me,' before staggering out to the kitchen.

Barbara was out in the garden and came in. She was annoyed because she had to reheat the Sunday roast, which had been ready four hours earlier. He had phoned from the pub earlier and said that he would be home in time for it.

Suddenly, there was shouting from both of them. She was standing her ground, which was very unusual.

I walked slowly to the kitchen doorway. She backed into a corner, standing up against the cooker. He was standing up close to her, shouting and pointing his finger in her face.

She picked up a saucepan of carrots from the cooker and threw it across the room. It hit the far wall next to me; I turned and looked at a large patch of water on the wall, as the droplets ran down the wallpaper. The carrots had stuck to the wallpaper, slowly sliding to their demise; the saucepan lay half tilted on the floor.

I remember her screaming, 'I'm not standing for this anymore.'

Dad quietened his tone and said to her, 'Hey, don't be like this, come on, it's you and me, it's OK, come here, give me a kiss.'

She reluctantly said, 'No.'

He said, 'Come on, you love me, give me a kiss.'

She didn't want to fight anymore, you could see she'd had enough. She just wanted dinner. So, with that, she leant in for a kiss. Without a second's hesitation, Dad leant his head back and intentionally head-butted her straight on the nose. Instantly, there was blood everywhere. She screamed so loudly, it sent chills through me. I stood there in shock, staring. It felt like everything was in slow motion. There was blood on her face, on her chin, her top, on his face, on the cooker, the sink. I couldn't move, I couldn't scream, I couldn't cry, all I could do was just stare. It felt like my whole body was paralysed. The only thing that worked was my eyes.

He stood there laughing. She pushed him back with one hand and grabbed a tea towel with the other and held it over her nose. She came charging towards me and grabbed my arm, shoving me towards the front door.

I stumbled as she pushed me out of the door. The tea towel was a mass of red by now. She took it away from her face enough to say, 'Run to Sarah's house NOW.'

She hurried behind me, pushing me towards the neighbour's house. I banged on their door. Sarah let us in and Barbara shouted at me to go upstairs and play. I went upstairs and hid under Sarah's bed. I don't remember what happened after that.

CHAPTER FOUR
My Seventh Birthday

Age 7

I t was my seventh birthday. Birthdays only meant one thing: Barbara and Dad would try to be on their best behaviour, and if I was lucky, I might get an Easter egg. My birthday was around Easter, so they were always in the shops at that time. I loved getting an Easter egg, with big, thick chocolate and a packet of sweets in the centre. Just the thought of an Easter egg made my heart swell, but sometimes, I got forgotten as well, but that didn't stop me thinking about the Easter egg. As usual, Dad had gone to the pub and Barbara was out – maybe getting her hair done or seeing friends. She went somewhere and I got left at the next-door neighbours' house, watching TV. The glamorous sounds and bright colours made my heart dance and I felt comfort in that. I liked being at the neighbours' house; the whole family loved each other and were really nice. They didn't shout or get angry, and they laughed together while watching the TV. They were very welcoming and were happy for me to stay there.

Just before 7p.m., Dad blasted the back door open with a white plastic bag in one hand, steadying himself in the doorway with the other. He was angry and started shouting at me to go home, so I scuttled out of the back door and across their patio, opening the back gate to our garden. As I went into the house, I could hear him following behind me. The back gate slammed menacingly and he staggered into the kitchen.

He opened the plastic bag. Inside was a takeaway he had brought home for dinner. He slammed the plates down on the glass dining table. As he started to put the food onto the plates, he mumbled something about being thrown out of the pub.

I sat down before being told to, scared of what would happen.

He looked at me across the table. 'Eat,' he gruffed.

I said I had already eaten at the neighbour's house earlier.

'EAT!' he said, staring at me with those dark brown eyes, like a predator about to pounce on its prey. He put his plate down opposite me and started to eat. He rammed food in his mouth like a savage, as if he hadn't eaten for days. There were bits of rice caught in his beard as he shovelled it in. I looked down at the yellow curry – big chunks of chicken and a mountain of rice. I didn't feel a tiny bit hungry, but I knew better than not to do as I was told. I picked up my fork and gently scooped some up. It was so spicy that I almost gagged, but I swallowed it anyway. I looked up. He was watching me intently. I put down my fork and before I could catch my breath, he lunged forward and came at me, scooping up my food on his fork with one hand while grabbing my hair with other, pulling it hard and forcing my head backwards. He rammed the fork in my mouth as hard as he could. I felt the stabbing pain of hard metal as the prongs touched the back of my throat. The shock made me gag hard.

He shouted in my face, 'YOU FUCKING EAT WHEN I TELL YOU TO EAT.'

He shouted those words four more times. I threw up on the plate. He stopped, put his fork down, and stood over me, staring down at me. As I looked up at him, I could feel a dribble of sick running down my chin. Petrified, eyes watery, I start to say, 'I'm...' but his big fist came crashing down on my mouth and nose. I flew off the chair and onto the hard-tiled floor. This was followed by another hard blow. My head banged against the floor, then darkness.

CHILD AND FAMILY CLINIC

16th March, 1990

Senior Social Worker,
Social Services Dept.,

Dear ███████████

Child's early history is complicated. In summary, Mr. explained that in Child's first year he had primarily looked after Child whilst her biological mother had often been out. She abruptly decided to leave Mr. when Child was approximately 1 year old to go off with another man and took Child with her. Mr. has no idea whatsoever what happened to Child in the next 2 years He had heard various rumours that child had been passed "from pillar to post" and of her being neglected but he had no concrete information. He had fought with the courts to get access to Child but before the situation was resolved, quite unexpectedly Child was left on paternal grandmother's doorstep a few days before her third birthday. Some months later Mr was awarded sole legal custody with mother apparently not even wanting access. She has had no contact since. Child has never talked about "her other mummy". Mr. and Mrs. have now been together for 5 years and therefore took on the job of looking after child.

My initial impression of Mr. and Mrs. was that both seemed very committed to child despite the very considerable difficulties in looking after her. The strain was quite clearly telling on Mrs. she acknowledged that she had been depressed for some months. At the Clinic child was inappropriately friendly with me, constantly chatting and interrupting as I talked with all three family members. She played with one thing after another but none with sustained interest, keeping all the time on the go. She showed all the characteristics of a child who has been severely emotionally deprived in early years and with the above history I was obviously concerned about the possibility of sexual abuse. I was quite open with Mr. and Mrs. about my concerns and raised the possibility of such abuse with them. They repeated that they had no idea what had happened to child from the age of 1 to 3 years but felt quite sure that there had been no possibility of abuse in the time that they had been looking after her. I conveyed to Mr. and Mrs. that I shared their very appropriate anxiety about child 's safety and was concerned about her future development. It seemed unlikely to me that child would be able to manage in main-stream schooling if there was no further therapeutic input. To this end father and step-mother agreed with my suggestions: that I see child for an individual assessment on 23rd February 1990, that I visit child 's school and they agreed to check out any possibility sources of Information to track down what had happened to child in earlier years.

Mrs. phoned the Clinic on 15th February 1990 to cancel my individual appointment with child. She told one of the secretaries, at the Clinic that her husband had changed his mind and didn't want child to go anywhere. I wrote to Mr. and Mrs. on 26th February 1990 stating my concern about child and my view that she would run into further problems if there were no further input. I made it clear that I would be happy to see child again if they reconsidered the matter. I have had no reply.

I would have liked to have had the opportunity to share with Mr. and Mrs that I would be contacting you but not had any answer, however think it's important you are made aware of the situation, particularly in the event of you receiving any further information in the future. Please do get in touch if you have any further queries.

Yours sincerely

Senior Psychiatric Registrar

copies to Dr. ███████████ ██████████
            ████████████ Health Visitor

MY SEVENTH BIRTHDAY

Conversation re. Child ███████

Child's mother left father when she was about 18 months old and she looked after child until she was about 3 when she deposited her on dad's doorstep then left. She has not been seen since. Stepmum is an over-dramatic lady. Threatened to leave the home, also to make child a ward of court. There have been particular problems at home recently and stepmum has been into school about 3 times this week. her blaming child who is quite demanding and very wound up. A bright child but calls out and takes up a lot of time and attention. Stepmum was heard to say 'he's gone too far this time (meaning dad). There was a science outing; child was ill in the night and not able to go. Mum attends a day centre for stress once a week, teacher unsure where this is. Parents went to the C&F Clinic - doctor came into the school to see MR but he couldn't remember what had been said. Dr was the psychiatrist involved. She was particularly concerned about child. When the family went to the Clinic, sexual abuse came up quite a lot. Dad won't go back now. Child is in a high state, has bright ideas but needs a lot of reassurance. Rarely speaks about home. One Monday she was particularly sad, said that mummy is going to pack her bags and go. Dr wanted me to come in and see child. I said it sounded like Social Services ought to be involved to support mum. I suggested if mum is having access to counselling, could tell her that she can go back to the C&F Clinic even if dad won't go. Failing that, in a crisis. Social Services would be able to help. Mum seems to give two different messages to child she calls her child and keeps her small

23

but blames her for the things that have gone wrong between her and the father. The family are under threat of eviction at the moment.

There was recently a row in the house over collection of tickets for the FA cup, when Mrs had a black eye and bleeding nose. There were concerns as to how much child witnessed/ witnesses violence at home. Certainly in school the following day child was aggressive and violent towards her peers. child was also saying that she wanted to die.

I asked about school, she is now a 1st year junior and she drives the teacher up the wall, teacher has been off for some of the term. Headteacher said it's interesting to see how she copes. There may well have been a slight improvement, head is getting a small amount of welfare help for her. Dr sees child twice a week, I think this is a form of counselling, but the headteacher was reluctant to clarify this. Child's father still drinks heavily, neighbours have rung social services when concerned. There has been a case conference and she is amenable. Teacher has been quite sharp with her on occasions, to which she responded positively.

I went to observe child – she was in the top junior class, who were operating a system of pals and minders, where each child is paired with an older top junior, 8-9 year old, and they do topic work with them. Child was sitting on a table with 5 boys, this was apparently working well but they were only grouped together because they had been the ones left over. She was out of her seat quite a lot going up to teacher for direction and support. On task. Teacher handled her very well, giving clear messages and encouragement. Fairly quiet but enjoying what she was doing. This particular teacher didn't find her a problem at all.

Stepmum, husband and child have been to C&F Clinic, saw Dr. Dad took exception. Child's only reference was she was lucky to have two mummies, her own mummy would be back soon. child didn't mention her background during our conversation. Stepmum v. concerned by the way child can just form relationships. It's thought she hasn't seen her gran since about 7 months old. Father was apparently quite shocked when she turned up on the doorstep. On night shifts so doesn't see a lot of her he considers that(stepmum) is the major figure in child's life.

Stepmum finds child quite difficult to handle. it's evident dads in the background in the situation.

I asked about when she had felt she would leave - child had been playing up for weeks and she rang up dad to say she had had enough. They had tried to split up about 18 months ago, dad moved out with child then came back. She is now saying she is not going to leave. She loves child dearly, but needs support and a break occasionally.

Stepmum is pleased with the time and effort school have put into child so far. A doctor suggested medication but I don't think this was taken up. Child is sometimes constipated, then opposite.

She saw Dr. Child emptied her desk, leading her to the conclusion that she had emotional/ behavioural difficulties. Child may still be under City Hospital.

WHAT NOBODY KNEW

School doctor suggested giving child a good smack from time to time.

I asked about the gran child was going to stay with. This is dad's mum who makes promises but doesn't keep them. Child isn't going for a whole month, maybe just a weekend. Dad isn't helpful towards stepmum's difficulty in coping with child, he sometimes doesn't believe her.

The previous day when dad was around and child was misbehaving, he told her off, I thought it was good that he had taken control.

Stepmum is very concerned that child goes off with men. She is not shy and goes off.

Recently on a trip to the zoo she wandered off 6 times with different people.

It seems appropriate to have a meeting with dad in school after 4pm on Monday or before 10.30 in the morning. Mum gave permission to talk to Dr. School described that Dr said the parent brought up abuse, parents told school Dr had brought up abuse as a possibility. Anything could have gone on before child was with dad.

Session with child ███████████ **School   30.4.90**

I observed child in Assembly. She has long plaited hair. Sat at the back sucking her thumb very close to another girl. A lot of hitting & elbowing going on. Teacher told her off and she behaved for a. while. Teacher prompted her to behave by saying she was sure child could show another pupil how to behave well. Each time she was addressed by teacher she put her thumb in. She was very physical, very excitable. Raised questions of possible abuse in my mind. Certainly emotionally insecure. I wanted to know more of her real mum, wondered if there was a chance of liaising with the Clinic.

Child's teacher described her as having an excellent memory, although when asked about home she clams up. Before Easter behaviour was terrible, has been marginally better. She said she is going to be spending a month in June with her Nan. but this turned out not to be so. Her stepmother told teacher she stands on an upstairs windowsill threatening to jump. Family are under threat of eviction. At home are stepmum and dad and child, Welfare support might be appropriate. Child had been noticeable since she first attended although behaviour seems to be becoming more intense. Relationship making is immature. Very messy. She has requested to eat on her own. Family are considering food allergy. Work capacity excellent, she reads very well. Number work possibly a bit below average. Doesn't work well on her own. Tends to bother others. Behaves like a 2-3 year old sometimes.

I chatted to her teacher at breaktime. When we went back to the classroom child was waiting for teacher. Feigned a headache. Sat in the classroom, then shot out without asking, holding her head. When out of teacher's vision she skipped to the toilet, came back with a tissue held to her head. Teacher was surprised child hadn't come up to me, she usually makes a beeline for any adult. She did ask who I was. She was happy to talk to me on a one to one. She darted around, full of questions, very vocal. She knew her age, birthday, could write address. Lives at home with mum, dad and 2 cats Mac and Arthur. At school likes maths & reading. Told me that in June she'll be staying with Grandma a long way away and going to school there; it's dad's mum and she be going on her own. She wanted to stay with her nan because she gives her lovely cuddles. At home she enjoys books colouring, child Doesn't like tidying her bedroom or getting bitten by the dog (one that visits). She has nightmares and used to fall out of bed.

On a one to one she was find although didn't give much away. I asked if she had 3 wishes what they would be. The first was to cuddle beetle juice, a man on TV with scruffy hair; second to have a house of her own and do her own thing, third to cuddle 2055 teddies, then changed to 3055 teddies. She then said could she have a fourth wish, for a cat, a dog, a mouse and a wizard who would give her anything she said.

My overall feelings were that child was emotionally immature, having difficulty making appropriate relationships with peers. Very needy for adult attention. Emotionally demanding, full of energy and full of questions. Quite difficult to handle.

MY SEVENTH BIRTHDAY

When I met with mum she asked how she had been because apparently she had said in the morning I don't feel like being naughty today. Mum is stepmum who I believe married dad but I got the impression she isn't being very supported by father in bringing up his child. Between the ages 16 months - 3 years child was with her real mother in Yorkshire. Dad left his first wife in October and fought for access but only saw her for 20 min when she was about 20 months old after a court order then not till she was about 3 when she was dumped on gran's doorstop with no toys or clothes. Her real mum said she was going shopping and it was the last they saw of her. She has now gone through the courts so she doesn't have to see child again. She has been with dad and stepmum since then. Little or no contact with mum since then, child didn't cry for her. Mum was then living at Yorkshire maybe still there. There have been abusive phone calls, possibly from her. Natural mother has an older child, who at the age of 8 asked if she could go and live with her father.

CLINICAL PSYCHOLOGY SERVICES FOR CHILDREN

12 November 1990

Social Worker

Dear ███████████

Re: Child (4.3.83)

I apologise for the delay in writing to you following our last telephone conversation on 1 November.

I saw child and Mrs at home three times during the summer holidays, starting on 2 August. At that time Mrs was very pleased with child and was not really finding her difficult to manage. She felt the change to a low sugar diet had been beneficial. Since child's return to school, however, I gather that her behaviour has significantly deteriorated again. I have visited 4 times from 14 September to 12 October and a behavioural programme involving stickers and brief time-out was begun on 5 October. During my visit on 12 October Mrs said she felt there was some mileage in the approach even though she also agreed with my basic approach that help from the Child and

Family Clinic was likely to be more worthwhile. However, child's father has refused to allow her to attend the Clinic, as you know.

A further visit was arranged for 19 October and cancelled that morning by Mrs. When we spoke on 1 November you were able to tell me what you believed had been happening and we agreed that I would write to MRS to see whether she wanted another appointment. In fact Mrs spoke to me by telephone on 2 November to say that she felt it was a waste of my time to visit again and that she would try to persuade Mr to change his mind over allowing her to go to the Child and Family Clinic. I do hope this step can be taken as I believe it will be of the utmost benefit to child

I am sorry I was unable to effect a significant change.

Best wishes,

Yours sincerely

███████████

███████████████████████

Consultant Clinical Psychologist

▓▓▓▓▓▓▓ SOCIAL SERVICES DEPARTMENT Client's surname: ▓▓▓▓▓▓

Index No.:

Team: ▓▓▓▓

DETAIL RECORD
for *specified* contacts, incidents or cases agreed with Senior

CLIENT

Surname ▓▓▓▓▓▓   **Forenames**

Address (current) ▓▓▓▓ ▓▓▓▓   **Telephone**

Address (home)   **Telephone**

Date of event 21/12/90

T.C from headmaster.

Concerned that we are aware of situation. Last week he had T.C. from Blank Text to tell him Mrs, child's stepmother, had walked out and is concerned that child is alone with her father and as he works nights is being "farmed out" to different people, and does not appear to be being cared for properly also her behaviour has been disturbed this past week.

Recorded by   Job title

Date

Date of event 21/12/90

Informed S.S.W of above which he was aware and understands that Mrs. has come back to the home now.

Recorded by   Job title

Date

CHAPTER FIVE
Bin Men

Age 7

I don't remember Christmases and birthdays much because we never had any money for presents – Dad drank it all. The only memory of a present I have is when I was quite young, age seven. That Christmas morning, I opened a present. It was a big, yellow teapot with little people inside, like a doll's house. The top spun, and when you opened the front door, it turned into stairs, and the back door opened to reveal two different living sections. I loved it. It was the best thing I had ever seen in my life.

Every night, Barbara would tell me to pick it up and put it away, along with my soft toys. She said if I didn't, she would pick all my toys up herself, put them in a black bag and put them out for the bin men. I would pick them up some nights, and other nights I didn't. Then, one night, Barbara told me to pick my toys up and I didn't, or I forgot, so she picked them up and stuffed them in a black bag and took them outside, telling me that the bin men would take them. I protested and asked her to bring them back inside, but she told me that if

I wanted them then I should have picked them up. I protested and cried but she took them out anyway.

The next morning as I woke up, I could hear the dustbin men outside our windows. Barbara rushed to put clothes on and get downstairs as quick as she could, but the bin men had already gone, along with my yellow teapot and my soft toys. I stood at the top of the stairs as she came back panting, saying, 'I told you the bin men would take them.'

I was crushed. The coolest toy in the world. Gone.

I don't think she did it on purpose, I think she was trying to teach me a lesson to make me pick up my toys.

Either way, there were two lessons learned that day. She learnt if she was going to threaten chucking out my toys, she needed to bring them back in before the bin man actually came and took them. I learnt that the world was cruel, and that I needed to pick my toys up if I wanted to keep them.

CHAPTER SIX
2a.m.

Age 8

During the week, Dad used to work night shifts, loading packages onto the backs of lorries. The pay was good and he didn't mind working through the night. He would come home and sleep during the day, so we had to creep around the house in fear of waking him, which I had accidentally done before and paid the price.

When he woke up at 4p.m., he would come down to eat his dinner and then head off to work. For that brief period when we saw him, he barely spoke. That was the thing with him; when he was sober, he would barely speak. He would acknowledge you, make light conversation, or speak when he had to, but overall, he was happy watching TV. He was completely different to the cocky, bold, loudmouthed tyrant he became when he was drunk.

I hated the weekends. At least in the week, I could escape to school. School was different. I liked words, painting and hanging upside down on the climbing frame, although I didn't have many friends. During the week, I walked on eggshells and hoped for the best, but at the weekend, who knew what was going to happen. He would come home on Friday morning, sleep until midday then get up and go straight to the pub. He didn't work Saturdays or Sundays, so they were pub days.

One weekend, I woke up in the middle of the night to him standing over my bed, nudging and poking me to wake up. The stale smell of beer and cigarettes wafted over me as I sat up and opened my eyes, which were stinging because I was too tired to be awake. He shouted, 'She's awake,' like it was a huge celebration. He said, 'I've got something to show you,' as he fell over my chair onto the floor. He tried getting up and fell back down, by which time, I had got out of bed and put my dressing gown on. Out of habit, I put my hand out to help him up, while he persistently told me he was not drunk and pressed his finger to his lips, motioning me to 'shush'.

He grabbed my chest of drawers with his free hand to climb back up. He walked to the doorway, indicating for me to go downstairs; at the top of the stairs, I saw the glow of the living room light and could hear loud voices. I went down the stairs and into the living room. Dad was behind me, shouting, 'Here she is.' I could see four men and two women, and Barbara, all drinking and talking. I felt nervous seeing all these people in our house.

Barbara looked at Dad and said, 'For goodness sake, it's 2a.m.! She shouldn't even be up.' He said it was fine, but she glared at him. 'No. She should be in bed.'

Dad started shouting, 'She's mine, I can do what the fuck I like with her. If you don't like it, I can soon change your mind.' When Dad was drunk, he wouldn't care what he said to Barbara, or how he said it.

He pressed down on my shoulder, firmly indicating for me to sit. I sat on the sofa, looking down at my cold, bare feet on the wooden boards of the living room floor. I was so tired. Dad picked up a can and started laughing with the people, pointing at me and saying, 'She looks just like me, doesn't she? We could be twins. She's mine and I love her more than anything in the world. If anybody ever touched her, I'd 'ave 'em.'

The people laughed along with him. A woman came over and stroked my hair and said, 'Oh you're sweet, aren't you? You have his eyes.' I didn't like her touching me, I didn't know her, I just wanted her to go away so I could go to bed.

They all carried on drinking for what seemed like a long time. I picked my feet up off the floor and tried to huddle them under my dressing gown for warmth. Dad took everyone except Barbara and me into the kitchen for more drinks. She sat there on the other side of the room, rolled her eyes at me and said, 'Just do what he says.' I was too tired to answer, so I just nodded.

Dad came back with wraps of paper and dumped one down in front of Barbara, and one next to me. I opened it up; it was pie and chips from the chip shop, stone cold.

Dad said, 'I brought you a present,' and stood there with his arms outstretched. 'Ta-da.'

Food was furthest from my thoughts, but I knew that you did as you were told, you had to play along. I picked up a greasy and unappetising cold chip and put it in my mouth and swallowed. Satisfied, Dad walked back to the kitchen and joined in with the banter. I couldn't touch the rest of the food; I just sat there hoping Barbara would say I could go to bed. Dad came back in to tell Barbara she was being rude to their guests. Sensing trouble, she got up and made her way to the kitchen. Dad looked at me and with a cheery smile and said, 'Eat up.' I nodded at him and looked down at the food, as he walked off.

While they were in the kitchen, all I could do was stare at the wall where our old-fashioned gas fire was. I took my feet out of the cosiness of my dressing gown and put them down on the cold floor. I could see a slight gap at the top of the fire from where I was sitting and decided to investigate. I went over and discovered quite a wide gap, all the way along the back of the fire, separating it from the wall, but not massively noticeable unless you were looking for it.

I glanced over at the kitchen door, which was just slightly open, and could hear Dad laughing and talking. I flited back to the sofa and grabbed a handful of chips. I put my hand up to the gap and started to wedge the chips down. They disappeared and suddenly, I felt like all my problems had been solved. I hurried back for the rest of the food, knowing that if I got caught doing this, well, it didn't bear thinking about. I posted the chips one after the other as fast as I could. Some were harder than others and needed some squashing to get them to go down, but all I was thinking was to do it as quickly as I could. I could feel my heartbeat in my throat; I was terrified of getting caught. I could hear him just the other side of the kitchen door, which had been pulled to but not completely closed.

Now the pie, but it wouldn't fit. I had to make it fit. I broke it up slowly, trying not to make a mess as it crumbled. I put it over the hole and kept pushing as hard as I could, watching it break into smaller pieces as it crumbled into the gap. I crushed it until every piece of evidence was gone. Then it was done, it was gone. I felt a massive sense of achievement as I sat back down, carefully taking the paper it was wrapped in with me. I felt like I had won for once and could feel my heart pounding. The adrenaline and fear made me feel out of control. My whole body was booming in tune with my heartbeat.

I sat back down, took a deep breath and tried to calm down. Eventually, I could feel my heart rate slowly coming back to normal and the fear lessening. I looked over at the door one more time. I could hear Dad's voice, loud and excitable as he told a story. I started to feel really tired, my eyelids were heavy. I tried desperately to keep my eyes open but I couldn't. Sleep took over.

When I opened my eyes, my face was wedged into the chip paper and I could feel the grease that had re-homed itself on my skin. I was still on the sofa, still in my dressing gown, and my feet were still cold. I sat up and saw a man and two women asleep in a heap on the living room floor. I looked towards the kitchen. The door was fully open and Dad was passed out on the kitchen floor. I couldn't see Barbara, so I got up to see if maybe she had gone to bed. Treading carefully and quietly, so as not to wake the floor bodies, I got to the living room door to see another man passed out on the stairs. I decided against trying to get past him and crept back to the sofa, away from the chip paper this time, and just lay there waiting. I must have fallen back to sleep because when I woke up, the people who were on the floor and stairs were all talking in the living room, trying to be polite, though they seemed embarrassed and awkward, completely different to how they were hours before. Dad barely spoke, which I guess made them more uncomfortable. One of them acknowledged that I was awake by giving me a baby wave. Barbara sat in her chair with her back to me, smoking. The people quickly said their goodbyes and headed out the front door. Dad sat down in his chair, lit up a cigarette and put the TV on. I got up and took myself to my bedroom. Exhausted and alone, with no explanation or apology, I was grateful for my own bed.

ADDITIONAL INFORMATION

ARE THERE ANY OTHER FACTORS WHICH YOU FEEL ARE RELEVANT TO YOUR CONCERN?

* The Home background is very unstable. Father is drinking again and showing violence to Mrs. ▮.

HAVE THE PARENTS BEEN APPROACHED ABOUT YOUR CONCERN? YES/~~NO~~

HAVE THEY AGREED TO S.P.S. INVOLVEMENT? YES/~~NO~~

WHAT IS THEIR VIEW OF THE CHILD'S PROBLEMS?

Mother is concerned — Father refuses to recognise the problem.

WHAT EFFECTS HAVE YOU NOTED?

Little change

HOW WOULD YOU LIKE THINGS TO CHANGE?

As the home environment is the cause of her emotional state — a boarding school might be appropriate.

WHAT DO YOU HOPE TO GET FROM THIS CONSULTATION?

Help for child & her mother (Stepmother) (Soc/Services)

REASON FOR REFERRAL AND IMMEDIATE ACTION

WHAT NOBODY KNEW

MRS IS WORRIED ABOUT CHILD. HER HUSBAND IS ON A "BINGE" AS WELL AS BEING ILL AND REFUSING TO SEE A DOCTOR. SHE WORRIED ABOUT HIS LACK OF INTEREST IN CHILD AND WHAT WOULD HAPPEN IF HE WERE TO DIE, OR BECOME UNBEARABLE FOR HER TO LIVE WITH THUS CREATING A PROBLEM OF WHO LOOKS AFTER CHILD. MRS WANTS TO BE RESPONSIBLE FOR CHILD. SHE ALSO THINKS THERE IS A MULTIDISCIPLINARY MEETING PLANNED THAT SHE KNOWS NOTHING ABOUT. MR IS VIOLENT TOWARDS HER.

CHAPTER SEVEN
Bed Incident

Age 8

I t was another late night/early morning binge. It had become a regular thing by this stage. They would happen constantly now. I woke up to the front door crashing open and Dad falling over as usual, talking loudly and being rowdy. I could hear this from my bed as always. I laid on my back with the covers over my mouth and nose, peering at my door, which was ajar. I never knew what was going to happen, but something always did.

I heard Barbara carrying him up the stairs, swearing at him, but couldn't make out what she was saying. They stopped outside my bedroom door. I could see the shadows of her feet under my door and hear her trying to catch her breath. She dragged him into their bedroom, which was right next to mine, and I heard her throw him on the bed. Then the *thud thud*, as she took his shoes off and they fell to the floor.

I felt relieved that I hadn't been disturbed, grateful that the whirlwind of drama didn't make it to my room for once. It seemed every week, Dad was drinking and coming home and making a scene, shouting, falling over, hitting Barbara. It seemed more like routine now because it was more and more constant. The midnight madness is what I called it. For months, Dad had developed a habit of coming home from the pub and falling through the front door, waking Barbara and I, singing, shouting, being aggressive, and then he would just pass out.

It went quiet, so I guessed that Barbara and Dad had gone to sleep. Their light went out and I snuggled down under the covers.

But some time later, my bedroom light came on; the sheer brightness made me sit up. Barbara was shouting and swearing, 'He fucking pissed the bed everywhere, all over himself, everything's soaked. Help me with him,' she said, as she grabbed s fresh sheet from the airing cupboard in the corner of my room. She also picked up a towel to cover him so he was semi decent.

I got out of bed ready to help her and we walked into their bedroom. I helped her lift him onto the floor. He was really heavy, like a dead weight, but he didn't wake at all, so we just stepped over and around him as we undid and remade the bed. Next, we hauled him onto the bed. He stirred, but not enough to wake up.

She looked at me when we were finally finished and told me to get back to bed. But I was awake now and my head was buzzing with adrenaline from having to lift him. I turned the light out in my room and made my way back to my bed. As I got into bed, I hoped tomorrow would be a better day, even though I knew it wouldn't be.

I closed my eyes and was just cosy enough to fall asleep when she stormed into my room again shouting, 'Bastard! Fucking bastard, he has done it again, he has pissed the bed again and this time on me as well, I'm soaked. I've had it up to here,' she gestured. 'I shouldn't have to put up with this, I've had enough.'

Barbara often threatened to leave us, and had actually done so before. I didn't care if she left or didn't; she would always threaten it and I think most of the time, it was for effect or attention. It was times like this, when things really kicked off, that really worried me, because this was usually what made her leave.

She went and got more sheets from the airing cupboard. I started to get out of bed but she shouted at me, 'You stay the fuck where you are. Go to sleep, this doesn't concern you.'

I got back under the covers as she told me to, watching her over the top. This time, my door was wide open; she had not shut it behind her after she bowled out of it. My bedroom light was out and her light was on, which made it feel more eerie. I was stiff as a board waiting for something to happen. I knew she was angry and I could feel that it wasn't over. From experience, usually when you thought it was over, it was far from it. She came out of their bedroom and switched the bathroom light on; the bathroom was directly opposite my room. She went back to their bedroom and there was silence as the minutes passed.

Suddenly, she was angrily dragging him under his arms to the bathroom, his face down towards the floor with the top of his head in her stomach. He was completely naked. She dragged him and dropped him next to the bath. I lay there motionless, waiting for it all to unfold. She stood there looking over him, panting and trying to get her breath back. Then, with all her might, she picked him up in one go and dropped him in the empty bathtub. She grabbed one of the soiled sheets from their bed and threw it over him, followed by the words, 'Sleep well, you fucker.' She turned out the bathroom light, stood in my doorway and boomed goodnight at me. She pulled my door to, but left it ajar.

Her light went out and the house was dark. I lay there, fearful. I didn't know what was going to happen next. *Should I go to sleep or shouldn't I?* I was so tired, but at the same time, worried something would happen. There was silence for a while, so I rolled over, pulled the covers up and shut my eyes. The next thing I heard was Dad vomiting on himself. I pulled the covers up over my head and wished I was somewhere else.

BED INCIDENT

Mr. is still reluctant to talk about child's mother and sees little point in this although does understand that child may see sane comparisons with her natural mother leaving and Mrs leaving when there have been marital problems.

The family have had an awful lot of difficulties including the threat of eviction which is why they have moved elsewhere. They are on the Child & Family waiting list. There are obvious taboos in the family, child never asks about her natural Mother, when she has tried to in the past Dad changed the subject. When she was 7 she started asking again but stepmother says she never cried openly. Obviously difference between the two of them about parenting, discussed the importance of the uniform approach, setting limits appropriately and not letting child manipulate - all things that they have heard from other groups and from the Social Worker. Stepmother says that when Child came to them at about 3, she did not know what cuddles were, stepmother very worried because she will make inappropriate approaches to absolutely anyone and will cuddle them and sit on their lap whether male or female. Social Worker is doing some work with them on that and it is acknowledged that she does make herself very vulnerable. The family have had some involvement with DR and I have permission to write to her.

Later discussion with DR and we decided that the cuddling, sitting on laps of teachers was inappropriate and I suggested that she have a teddy to cuddle instead. Later heard from teacher that she has provided a teddy in school and this has been quite successful.

████████████

Educational Psychologist   16thJuly 1992

WHAT NOBODY KNEW

Parent's (or guardian's) current views about the child's special needs and the provision being made to meet those needs. (Please obtain/parent/guardian's counter signature to any comments recorded on their behalf and/ or attach any written comments submitted by them).

Child . desperately needs help in forming relationships both with her peers and adults.
She is a very destructive and disruptive child.
Since we moved in June **Child** output at school has deteriorated beyond belief. We expected some sort of backlash from her, but never nothing as drastic as this. Socially her behaviour is totally unacceptable and because of this we find ourselves prisoners in our home. Even there **Child** has great difficulty in accepting more than a one to one relationship. This certainly adds to the stresses of everyday living.
Child seeks, even demands 24 hr attention.

We as her parents feel that **Child** . needs a great deal of proffesional help in helping with her problems and are therefore requesting boarding school education for her. We ask this reluctantly because we are at the end of our resources. We are willing to seek help from the Child and Family Clinic.
She has lost most of her childhood and even if just a little bit of this can be saved for her we feel that it will be a great achiovment.

Signature ██████████████ (Head Teacher)   (Please continue overleaf if necessary)

Signature ██████████████   Date *10 11 92*
(Parent/Guardian)

CHAPTER EIGHT
Belt

Age 8

Sometimes, you feel most at peace when you're alone, when you're calm and tranquil. When your head is clear, you can try to understand the world better.

It's other people who cloud our judgement, who cause us to make rash or stupid mistakes. It's other people who hurt us, lie to us, and make us believe they are something they're not.

I had a lot of my time with my own thoughts because I spent a lot of time on my own in my room. My room was usually my safe place.

One day, that changed. I was alone and content in my room. Then the door flew open and crack went the belt as it hit me. I wailed with pain, my thoughts scrambled with fear and torment. Crack went the belt again, as a sharp, hard pain tore through my body. Tears fell from my face as I ran to the corner of the room and curled up in a ball, hoping to save myself. Multiple strikes, the burning pain taking over my whole body, my skin sweating from the terror; blow after blow without a second's pause. Then he dropped the belt, staggered out the door and down the stairs. The hum of the TV resonated through the floor.

I didn't move. I laid there, shaking uncontrollably, with trickles of blood running down my back. My body was a fireball of pain, shaking with shock. I tried to block out the pain and find my alone tranquil mindset again, but it had gone. This was the first time he hit me with an object. There was no explanation.

CHAPTER NINE
Dragon's Breath Mustard

Age 9

I always used to suck my thumb and twiddle my ear. I don't know why I did it, I just did. I liked it, it made me feel relaxed. When I felt uncomfortable, it seemed natural to put my thumb in my mouth. I don't remember when I first started doing it but it was one of the only comforts I had.

Barbara was constantly telling me to take my thumb out of my mouth or smacking it out of my mouth, but a lot of the time, I honestly didn't realise I was doing it.

Dad was at the pub as usual one day, and Barbara was depressed, so she decided we were going to Anne's house. Sometimes, if Barbara was depressed, she thought it was a good idea to get out of the house. Anne was her sister and lived a 15-minute bus ride away. I never liked Anne. She wasn't a very nice lady. If she came to our house when Dad wasn't there, she used to tell me to fuck off to my room. So I don't think she was a fan of me either.

When we arrived, Anne's front door was wide open and she was shouting at a man, telling him to go to hell.

The man was standing on the grass, calling her names and swearing at her. Barbara just walked into the house with me in tow, ignoring everything that was happening. The man stormed off, Anne closed the front door and came into the house and just rolled her eyes at Barbara.

Barbara gave a massive sigh and said, 'I've had enough. Can we talk?'

Anne looked at me and said, 'Is she still sucking her thumb?' She smacked my hand out of my mouth and said, 'What have I told you?' Then she turned to Barbara and said, 'I'll deal with her.' She got me by the scruff of the neck, dragged me through to the kitchen, put a dining chair in the middle of the kitchen floor, and said, 'Sit.'

Anne was a vicious woman who was very spiteful. I had seen her hurt people before so I sat. She walked over to the kitchen cupboards and took out a jar. She opened the jar, wafted it under my nose, and said, 'Smell that.' The vile smell went up my nose and immediately irritated my nostrils. She turned the jar upside down and stuck one of my thumbs in it, then the other one. I looked at my thumbs covered in the thick, gloopy substance. She smiled and said, 'Lick it.' I refused, but she said, 'Lick it now.' I really didn't want to, so I shook my head. She grabbed my left thumb and smeared it against my lips. As my lips started to burn, my tongue came out automatically to lick them. The instant hot sensation on my tongue and in my throat was intense. I started to blow out my mouth to try and cool my throat down. I got my sleeve and wiped at my lips like crazy. I hated the feeling and was frightened at what was going to happen.

Anne started laughing. She said, 'It's dragon's breath mustard. It's not very nice, is it?' Then she picked up the cat that was rubbing itself around the chair and put it on my lap, saying, 'This is your new friend, stroke it, now.' I tried to stroke it carefully without getting any mustard on it. Poor thing was innocent and I didn't want it tasting what I had just had to. But the mustard stuck to the cat's fur as it wanted more and more attention.

I looked up at Anne. She laughed in my face and said, 'Maybe next time, you will think twice about sticking your thumb in your mouth. You can stay sitting there till Barbara decides to take you home. That should give you enough time to think about what you've done.' With that, she left the room.

I sat there for hours; the cat got bored way back and went to find better things. I could hear the murmur of the two of them talking in the next room. My bottom hurt from sitting on the chair so long. I stared at my hands, thick with gloop and cat hair. I couldn't even scratch an itch on my face because the smell was so horrible. I sat there so long that when I looked up at the window, I could see it was really dark outside. It had been lunchtime when we arrived. It felt like I had been there for days.

Barbara finally came in and said, 'Get up, we're going home, and wipe that stupid, sad look off your face.'

I stood up to do as I was told. The kitchen sink was in front of me. She turned on the tap and said, 'While you're at it, wash that crap off your hands.'

My heart jumped. I put my hands under the water and tugged at my thumbs. They were stiff from being upright and covered in the gloop for so long, and it was a massive relief to get the horrible stuff off my skin and down the drain. I scrubbed harder and harder until, finally, my thumbs felt normal again.

As I was drying my hands, Anne came into the room and leered at me, her face right in mine. She said she really looked forward to seeing me again soon, and that she'd always have dragon's breath mustard in her cupboard just waiting for me. Then she said, 'Maybe one day, you will come and live with me. I'll sort you out good and proper.' I stared at her and she just kept staring back at me. I wanted to shout at her and hurt her for being nasty to me, but I couldn't. I was scared of what would happen if I did. Barbara gave me a shove and we left.

CHAPTER TEN
Chocolate

Age 10

Dad came storming into the living room. I was sitting cross-legged on the floor, watching one of my favourite films: *The BFG*. He grabbed the back of my neck with a claw-like grip, spun me up onto my feet, and then pushed my neck so hard that I fell and ended up sprawled, face-down on the hard floor. He grabbed me again, this time by my hair, and dragged me upright to a standing position. He turned me round to face him and said in a quiet but frightening tone, 'Where is my chocolate?'

I had no idea what he was talking about and couldn't think quickly enough after all the commotion. So, terrified and confused, my heart racing, I whimpered, 'I don't know.'

'I will ask you again, where is my fucking chocolate?' His voice was now even angrier, pushing up to me so I had to keep stepping backwards, and now he was right in front of my face.

I automatically stepped back away from him. I felt the wall bump against my back. I had nowhere to go. I put the palms of my hands against the wall to steady myself. Now he was staring at me with the burning, angry eyes.

'I'm not going to ask you again, this is your last chance.'

I didn't know what to do. I told him again that I didn't know, and I really didn't. I wished he would explain.

I looked past him and Barbara, who stood behind him, her hands in the prayer position motioning them to me, was mouthing the words, 'Please.'

Then, in a moment, it all made sense. She did it; she ate the chocolate. It was easier for me to take the brunt of her greedy ways than her, or maybe she just didn't feel like getting bashed today.

I didn't see the point of telling the truth. She had probably already told him I did it, hence the situation I was in. If I told the truth, Barbara would deny it, and I would get in trouble for supposedly lying.

He shouted at me, 'Don't look at her,' and then said, 'Well?'

I looked at him and could feel a lump forming in my throat, tears burning behind my eyes. I knew what was coming.

So, I let the words fall from my mouth. 'I did it.'

'That wasn't so hard, was it?' he said.

He turned to walk away, and I let out a silent sigh of relief, but in that millisecond, he swung around and punched me straight on my nose. The force of the blow knocked my head flying into the wall behind me. My head was swimming. Moments later, I could feel the watery blood on my face and the oily taste of it in the back of my throat.

I didn't get chance to think before he hit me again in the same place, right on my nose. This time, my legs collapsed under me. I was dazed and confused in a heap on the floor. As I looked up, his shoe came crashing down onto my face and more blood spilled out of my mouth. Then I couldn't see anything except tears and blood. A loud ringing noise pierced my ears, deafening me. I couldn't hear and I could hardly see, but I could just make him out. He was still standing above me, yelling down at my face and pointing his finger at me. He moved away, but then again, his shoe smashed into my face. I was already on the floor, but I slumped down, unable to do anything to protect myself. The last thing I remember is his foot coming down towards me again. After that, nothing…

I woke up in a hospital bed with a nurse standing over me. I had no idea how long I'd been there. As my eyes adjusted to the light, she said, 'Hello, that was a nasty fall you had. You dislocated your jaw and broke your nose. We gave you some strong painkillers. That's why your head might be feeling a little fuzzy right now. The doctor managed to put your jaw back while you were out, and we have stopped the bleeding. Your face is very swollen at the moment but don't be too alarmed.' I felt shocked at what she had said. I wanted to touch my face but daren't.

I tried to sit up and ask for a drink, but I couldn't open my mouth. The nurse said, 'The most important thing is that we have wired your jaw shut, mainly for the healing process. You must only have liquids for four weeks.'

She came towards me with a funny-looking plastic cup with a hole in it and a straw. She poked the straw into the side of my mouth. I managed to suck the water through it and she said, 'Hey presto.' She told me that I would be staying in overnight, just as a precaution.

Suddenly, the curtain that had sealed us off from everything was thrown open and Dad stood there. The nurse asked if he was family. He said, 'I am her Dad,' in his usual aggressive tone.

She said, 'OK, I will give you two some time alone.'

He walked over to my bed and just looked at me for a minute or two, not saying anything. I started to get scared and panic inside. If he was going to kill me, I couldn't scream, I would just have to die where I was. I'm sure he could see the fear all over my battered face. He leant into me, the side of his face pressed up against mine, the sharp pricks of his beard stabbing against my face. He whispered into my ear, 'You tell anyone what happened and things will get a lot worse for you than they are right now.'

Having delivered his threat, he sat on a chair on the other side of the room, folded his arms and just stared at me.

Suddenly, the curtain opened again and the same nurse was back. Relief took over my whole body. She told me that because of my age, being only 10, I had to stay in hospital with a parent, but the parent didn't have to stay in the same room if they didn't want to. She looked at Dad and he said, 'I'm staying right here.' He had his arms folded in a I'm-not-backing-down kind of way, which the nurse understood. She said that was completely fine, and started to tell him where he could get drinks and food.

It was already really late and the nurse asked if she could turn the main light off and put the night lights on. Dad said, 'Do what you want, we're not getting in your way.'

The night lights came on, which were like landing strip lights, but on the ceiling. I stared up at them, imagining a plane would come, pick me up and take me away. I lay there awake the whole night, occasionally looking over at him. He sat there the whole time with his arms crossed, watching me.

I couldn't sleep because of the fear of not knowing what he was thinking or what he was going to do.

When morning came, neither of us had slept or spoken the whole night, not that I could have spoken even if I had tried.

The nurse came round and helped me drink a soup, it was nice and warm, I was very grateful as I hadn't had a drink all night. Dad grunted at her, 'Are we done? I just want to take her home.' The nurse said she would speak to the doctor and try to hurry it along, and she told me that it was OK for me to get dressed.

I was very stiff moving from the bed. I don't know how many days I had been lying down for but it was like my body didn't want to move. I tried to take my gown off but it was tied around my neck and I couldn't speak to ask for help. Dad looked at me with disgust, got up and went out through the curtain. I felt so helpless trying to get the robe untied. My face was starting to ache and the one person who did this to me wouldn't even help. I sat on the bed, defeated, and started to cry. The next swish of the curtain was the nurse. She explained that Dad had gone to the main entrance to have a cigarette and call a taxi, and that he had told her to get me dressed. She undid the ties at the back and held them there while she passed me my T-shirt. I tried to get it over my head, but I couldn't do it; my nose was so swollen and all down the side of my face was so sore. She could see I was struggling and said, 'Let me help you,' widening the neck of the T-shirt and gently shimmying it over my face. She got my trousers and put them over my feet and I shuffled into them.

She crouched down to put my shoes on and stayed in that position once she'd finished with the shoes. She put my hands in hers, looked right into my face, and said, 'If someone did this to you, you can tell. You don't have to be alone. Did someone do this to you?' I looked at her. She had a kind face and seemed genuinely sincere, but Dad's words were echoing through my ears loud and clear. So, I looked at her and shook my head.

'Are you sure?' she said softly? Then, the curtain flew open again. This time, Dad nearly pulled it off its hooks.

'Come on! What's taking so fucking long?' he grunted.

The nurse touched my shoe and said, All done, you are ready to go,' as she stood up. I walked with my achy body over to Dad. He turned and marched away. I followed along behind. I looked back at the nurse just for a moment, and she gave me a kind smile.

'Come on and pick up the pace,' Dad growled at me loudly.

The taxi ride home was a silent one. I just stared out of the window. My whole body hurt from lack of food, sleep and the obvious.

As we walked in the front door, Dad threw what looked like pills at Barbara and said, 'She needs these.' He looked at me and said, 'You will be spending the next four weeks in your bedroom.' He pointed his finger at me, poking my cheek hard. 'If I hear a peep from you, there will be trouble.'

Dad turned to Barbara and said he was going to the pub. He pointed up the stairs and in a firm voice, he said to me, 'You, go.'

I was glad to be going to bed, I needed to sleep so much. I thought about trying to get my top off when I got to my bedroom and decided against it, so I stayed in my clothes and got into bed.

The next four weeks were nice and uneventful. I have no idea whether he left me alone because he was ashamed, embarrassed or just didn't care. All the same, I could still hear his drunken stupors downstairs, but he never came to my room for all that time. I felt quite at ease, which wasn't normal for me at all. I just had a radio in my bedroom and a few books, which was all I needed. I liked listening to the music; it made me feel like I was somewhere better. Different songs took me to different places. I would turn the knob on the radio to find different songs to entertain my day, then have a nice read of my books. Sometimes, Barbara wouldn't remember or couldn't be bothered to bring me soup or anything easy to swallow, which was hard at first, but the hunger pangs soon wore off if I drank a lot of water. I didn't have to worry about getting water because I could get it from the bathroom opposite my room. I learnt to angle my face just right under the tap so at least there was no chance of dehydration.

When she did remember to bring me something, it was normally cold by the time it got to me, but I was grateful all the same. I think I had been recovering at home for about two weeks by this point. The time had felt like it had flown by.

One day, I looked out of my bedroom window. It was a lovely, sunny day, and all the children were playing in the street, all looking happy chasing each other and kicking footballs. I wanted to join them, I wanted to play and have fun, but I was never allowed to play in the street. Then, from the corner of my eye, I saw Dad, drunk, staggering up the street, carrying a blue carrier bag. Instead of coming up the path, he stopped and walked over to the children. He opened the bag, took out chocolate bars and handed them to all the children. They all flocked to him. He was smiling and ruffled one little boy's hair and high-fived another. When the bag was empty, he put it in his pocket and headed for our front door. I stood there at the window, put my hand on my jaw and felt the tears cascade down my face. In that moment, I had never felt so unwanted in my whole life.

Two weeks later, it was the night before I had to go back to the hospital for them to unwire my jaw. It was going to be such a relief to be able to move my mouth properly. I lay in bed and got a book to read. Just as I started to read, the lights went out and the radio stopped – the electricity had run out. It happened quite a lot, usually because we had no money to pay it. Oh well, I thought. I put the book under my covers and went to sleep.

The next morning, Barbara took me to the hospital. Dad was in bed after working the night shift, so it was just me and her. We were in the hospital for a few hours. Barbara told the other patients waiting that I was a clumsy child and did these things to myself, and that she was my stepmother, and she didn't have to look after me all these years but she did because that's the sort of person she was.

Once everything was done, my jaw was back to normal. It felt amazing being able to move it again. It had felt like forever since I had done that. We caught a taxi outside and Barbara gave the driver the address. My newfound happiness had been crushed by a simple address: Anne's house.

Barbara rattled on the door. Anne opened it, looked at me, and said hello with a big grin on her face. I dug my hands deep in my pockets, remembering the last time. Barbara said, 'Get in,' and pushed me through the door. Anne took my hand and pulled me to the kitchen and put the chair in the same place. I sat down. I didn't struggle. I let her put the mustard on my thumbs. No cat in sight this time though. After all I had just been through, her degrading me like this was nothing. She looked at me and said, 'You're learning,' leant into me, pinched my face hard with her fingers and then walked into the other room.

I could hear them both talking, Barbara telling Anne the truth about what had happened to me and Anne saying that I deserved everything I got. I heard Barbara say that she was scared for her life. I was also scared, but I didn't see Barbara sitting and having a chat with me about it.

Anne said, 'Why don't you come and live with me? Leave the brat there, she is his child not yours, his responsibility. You're just babysitter. They are both nothing but trouble. The sooner you leave them, the better.'

They carried on talking while I sat there listening, confused as to why everyone was against me. Was she going to leave? Most importantly, was she going to leave me with my Dad who did this. Why did everyone hate me so much?

Barbara came in and told me to wash my hands. As we were leaving, Barbara told Anne that she would think about what she had said. We were about to head up the path when Anne poked me on the back of the shoulder and said, 'Hey.' I turned around to look at her. She said, 'Chin up,' and started laughing uncontrollably. Barbara smirked and started laughing too, before giving me a shove and saying, 'Come on, let's go.' She looked at Anne and said in a mocking tone, 'Before she starts crying.'

I felt like the lowest of the low, the bullied kid who has had its beating and is powerless against more bullies. While other people got cuddles when they got hurt, I got mocked and humiliated. I could feel the lump in my throat and the tears ready to break out of my eyes. But this time, I managed to hold it in. I wasn't going to give them the satisfaction of seeing me cry. I was broken enough for one day.

CHAPTER ELEVEN
The Pub

Age 11

A lot of times, I had to be left at the pub with Dad because there was no one to look after me. I was seven the first time. Barbara would just drop me there and say she had to do shopping. So I would be ushered into the corner of the pub, Dad telling me I wasn't allowed to be there and that I shouldn't be seen or heard.

I would have to sit on the floor under a table for a long time until he was ready to go or until Barbara came back and took me home, which was rare.

Once, I had sat there all afternoon and evening, everybody left the pub, the pub doors closed and still I stayed. It was quiet and dark. I wasn't sure what I was supposed to do, so I pulled my knees up closer to my chest and waited. Apparently, so I was told, Dad took a taxi home and Barbara thought I was lying under his coat in the back of the taxi and was calling my name. Only then did Dad remember that I was with him that day and he'd left me at the pub. He didn't have any more money for another taxi so he rang the landlord of the pub and asked him if he could he drive me home when he had a spare minute.

When I was 12 and off on school holidays, I had to sit in the pub with Dad a lot. I knew my little corner on the floor well. I would sit, knees up with my hands tightly around them, and watch the people. Occasionally, someone would crouch down and talk to me. I used to hate it – the smell of alcohol on their breath, their loud voices. I thought it was better to be left alone, as that's what I was used to. Dad would throw a packet of crisps or nuts at me occasionally and the barman, if he remembered or if Dad told him to, would bring me water or lemonade. I had no choice but to get used to it under the table. I'd pretend I was in a tent and all the people I was watching were like TV characters. I would look at their different ways of moving and talking. Some people would just listen to a conversation, others would roar and boom with their loud voices. Dad liked to tell stories and buy people drinks and pat people on the back. He knew a lot of people at the pub. I never saw him like this at home. It was like Jekyll and Hyde, a completely different person. Occasionally, a fight would break out and I would push myself as far back as I could so I didn't get hit by anything or anyone. Once, someone threw a glass in a fight and the glass smashed really close to me. It really scared me and I learnt to think quick after that.

I'd learnt to block out the sticky floors, stale beer and cigarette smells, along with anything else nasty that happened to be under the table that day; cigarette butts, maybe a rogue chip or some stowaway peas.

I wondered how, if I had the problems that people made out, I could I sit under a pub table with nothing to do for hours on end.

I always dreaded it when evening came. One night, Dad was steaming as usual, and barely able to stand. As he was leaving the pub, the barman shouted, 'Your daughter!' Dad came over and crouched on the floor, looking at me under the table. He said, 'Oh yeah, forgot about you, come on.' He staggered up, knocking chairs and glasses as he did, so I got up and headed out of the pub. It was dark outside and he would fall over everything in his path. He would even fall over himself.

It was late, dark and cold. It was half an hour's walk home for a normal, sober person, but with someone who's drunk, I knew it would take a an hour or longer. This wasn't the first time this had happened, so I knew it would be quite a while till we were home. There was no chance of a taxi, as he had drunk all his money. Even if he had any money, it was doubtful he would be able to see it properly, or be able to hold it without dropping it all over the floor like he once did. That time, he had lain on the ground trying to find it, before crawling along the path in the dark and deciding to lie down and sleep where he was. So I then had the mammoth task of trying to lift a sleeping drunk person double my size.

This particular night, I got what I dreaded all the way home: loud singing, lolling over me, trying to knock me over, trying to steal flowers from the buckets outside shops, peeing in doorways, falling over, laughing and giving me a hard shove every now and then. Then, when we got to the point where he said he couldn't walk anymore, he would throw his big, heavy arm around my neck and I would try to hold him up and keep walking towards home.

Once we were out of the town, the walk home was next to a busy road, and his body weight pushed into mine. He would push me into the road and would be talking nonsense while I was holding him up, trying to walk and push us back onto the pavement. I would see car lights coming towards us and they would beep their horns and swerve round us. Some people would shout things from their cars, but I couldn't move him out of the way. I was only young and I wasn't strong enough, so I prayed we didn't get hit. Sometimes, when a fast car came towards us, I would shut my eyes really tight because I didn't want to see it hit me. I'd open them with a jolt as the car slammed on its brakes and blared the horn. Dad was completely oblivious to all this, just slumped over me mumbling something.

I would give a sigh of relief when he swayed back over to the pavement and we were safe, but a mile down the road, it would happen again. And again. It was a relief when he used to fall over on the grass and lay there for 10 or 15 minutes. It would give me a chance to rest. My shoulders and back would be hurting from taking his weight and I needed that break to be able to keep going. As we neared home, it would be back to the loud singing again. I always thought to myself that our neighbours had seen me do this time and time again, and heard noises from our house and seen bruises. But nobody ever helped us. I suppose nobody wanted to get involved; it was easier for them to carry on as normal, like nothing was happening. At least not to them.

This time, when I got to our front door, it was locked so I banged on the door. I bent down with my hands on my knees, panting. I could finally breathe deeply. I had made it. God knows how long it took me, but I did it. I felt like I had just run a marathon and now I was over the finish line. Dad fell into the flowerbeds and just lay there. Barbara opened the door and asked where he was. I stood up and pointed whilst still trying to catch my breath. We picked him up, dragged him into the house and dumped him in his armchair. He fell straight to sleep. Barbara told me it was time for my bed and that I shouldn't be up this late. Not once did she ask me what happened, whether I was OK, or if I had had anything decent to eat. That's the way it always was. And so I would go to my room, exhausted. I always felt angry – every time, it was the same. Why did I have to carry him home? Why did no one ask how I felt, or if I was OK? Sometimes, you just have to do what you do.

THE PUB

COMMUNITY NHS TRUST

!"#$%&'()&*+,#$-&!./#! &

Name: Child

Address: ███████

Date of Birth: ███████

Date of Report: Dec. 1993

Dear ███████

Thank you for asking me to contribute to the review of child's statementing which I understand is primarily concerned with the whole question of secondary education.

I am enclosing a copy of my previous report to Dr. dated 20th May 1993 which outlines in some detail the background history together with the nature and extent of the Clinic's involvement.

I would now like to update that report, given my ongoing involvement with Mr. and Mrs. and child.

Shortly after writing my report in May 1993, the situation which had been improving suddenly deteriorated. This coincided with Mr collapsing and being rushed into hospital and child 's reaction, although understandable in the context of her worries about her father, placed enormous pressure on an already strained parental relationship manifested in worries over health, money and depression. In fact, Mrs. was at that stage again threatening to leave and child, although denying the importance of this, was clearly feeling unsettled.

Although things have since improved, they never quite returned to the point where the parents were really feeling in control of child it seems to me that child continues to have quite dramatic mood swings which demand considerable management and reinforcement which may be beyond the parents' abilities, given Mrs. own mood swings and also the fact that Mr. is now recovering from a major operation.

CHAPTER TWELVE
Videos

Age 11

Dad never regretted anything he did, drunk or sober. He just carried on as normal, like everything was as it should be. He would avoid us when he was at home by engrossing himself in sport on TV until it was pub time, then he would leave and spend the rest of the day there. I was always grateful when I didn't have to go to the pub and I could stay home.

I usually spent a lot of time in my bedroom, but if Barbara needed what she called 'a break', which meant she wanted to spend the day at a neighbour's while Dad was at the pub, she would call me down from my room and say I could watch videos on the TV downstairs on my own. She would leave me by myself and I would be so excited to be able to watch what I loved.

I would take my videos off the shelf and lay them in front of me, as I chose which adventure would I watch: *An American Tail, The BFG, Labyrinth, The NeverEnding Story, The Land Before Time* or *All Dogs Go To Heaven*. They were all my favourites. They had either been given to us or were recorded off the TV, in which case, the video had the previous recording scribbled out and the name of the film written over it.

The films made me feel special. It was like I was there, living the adventure with each and every one of them. If I had to choose the one I liked the most, it would be *The BFG*. Whenever I watched it, I hoped one day, the BFG would snatch me away and look after me. Life with him looked like so much fun, and he really cared about the little girl. Watching my videos was the only fun I ever truly had at home.

Dad liked watching films too. He would drag me out of bed at stupid o'clock and make me watch them with him after yet another night of drinking, the alcohol along with cigarettes on his breath wafting onto my sleepy face as he marched me downstairs and said, 'Sit on the arm of my chair and watch with me. If you fall asleep, I'll give you a smack.'

He liked watching martial art films. I grew to like them because they weren't as scary as some of his other favourites, and focused a lot on good versus bad. But then other times, he would make me watch really scary films like *An American Werewolf in London*, *Predator*, *The Shining*, *The Silence of the Lambs* and *A Nightmare on Elm Street*. I used to cover my eyes if I didn't like what I saw. The awful things in some of them would scare me. I was only 11 years old. He would mock me and say, 'What's the matter with ya? You're not scared, are ya?' And then, he would laugh loudly and pull my hands down from my eyes and tell me to stop being a baby and watch.

A few times, I had fallen asleep on the edge of the chair and he would push me hard off the arm and I would hit the floor heavily. He would then say, 'Now get up and watch the film properly.'

Towards the end of a film, the alcohol would prove too much for him and he would fall asleep in the chair. I knew my cue and would climb the stairs back to my bed. I would lie there sometimes, too scared to sleep because of what I had just seen. I would replay it in my head, too frightened to shut my eyes.

The next morning, I would always find him in the same position I had left him, with the TV buzzing away where the film had stopped. Barbara would come down, oblivious to what I had seen the night before.

The images used to haunt me for days, but I daren't show that I was scared. I knew better than that.

PART TWO

SCHOOL AND TEENAGE MEMORIES

CHAPTER THIRTEEN
Shipped Off

Age 11

Behavioural problems they called it.

Allergy to sugar.

Hyperactivity.

Disruptive child.

Learning difficulties.

Poor social skills.

This was before ADHD and proper diagnoses were heard of.

'Let's send her to a special needs school, that should fix her.'

I had already been to quite a few schools, although I was off regularly, whenever I'd been hit, so I wasn't too bothered about going to another one. However, my problems were actually all down to bad parenting. Barbara and Dad were delighted when I got shipped off to a special needs boarding school. It meant I would only come home for 12 weeks a year. Dad could drink as much as he wanted, and could beat up Barbara as many times as he felt like it. Barbara didn't have to look after me, so she was as free as a bird to do what she wanted when she wanted. They were stripped of their parental rights free of charge. Pass the buck; let someone else deal with the damage they had caused. What they didn't realise was that they were damaging me more, if that was possible. Sure, I was free of the beatings, but it opened my eyes to a world where people genuinely had severe problems. I was thrown in amongst them for good measure.

Open to.

Education
Director of Education

Hertfordshire
COUNTY COUNCIL

FAX   :
Telephone   :
Please ask for   :
My ref   :
Your ref   :

Date 5 October, 1994

Dear ▮▮▮▮

1981 EDUCATION ACT
CHILD'S NAME: Child   DATE OF BIRTH: ▮▮▮▮
ADDRESS: ▮▮▮▮▮▮▮▮▮▮

Thank you for letting me know that a place is available at ▮▮▮▮ School
for Child from 4 October 1994.

I confirm that, subject to approval by the Secretary of State in accordance
with Section 11 3(b) of the Education Act 1981, the ▮▮▮▮ County
Council Education Department will accept financial responsibility for
Child's education at ▮▮▮▮ School under the Authority's arrangements
for the placement of children with special educational needs.   Accounts
should be sent to the Director of Education ▮▮▮▮.   It would also
be helpful if we could receive copies of school reports, details of holiday
dates etc., these should, please, be sent under the reference ▮▮.

I am grateful to you for the offer of this place for Child and I hope that
she will soon settle in with you.

Yours sincerely,

Special Educational Needs Officer
Parent and Student Services

cc

CHAPTER FOURTEEN
Greenwood

Age 11

I was 11 when I got shipped off to an all-girls boarding school for children with learning difficulties. I was so scared, as I travelled for two hours alone in the back seat of a taxi. The driver said nothing, he just had the radio station on to keep him company, though I could barely hear it. I looked out the window, but could only see green scenery or motorway, so nothing really to see or enjoy. I was nervous because I didn't really understand what was happening. I couldn't understand why yesterday, I was in my bedroom and Barbara and Dad were being nice. They were *never* nice. Then that morning, they said goodbye to me, and there I was. I was told I was going to live at school, but that was about it. It was roughly 11a.m.

The car pulled up to a big, old Victorian school building. I remember up on the brickwork, which towered above me, there was a stone, engraved with the numbers 1913. There were lots of windows everywhere, and my eyes flitted to each one to see if I could see any movement.

A lady came out, very smartly-dressed in posh high heels, a woollen skirt and a white shirt. She had well-kept short hair and a confident walk about her. She told me she was the head teacher, and that she was going to show me around the school and take me to where I would be staying. She stood beside me, we both looked up at the building, and she held out her hand. I looked at it, not sure what to do, then she gently took my hand and said, 'Come on, let's go.' She waved the taxi driver off with the other hand and we walked in together. She seemed very kind, but I was still apprehensive. She was a stranger to me.

As I stepped through the doors, there was a girl, maybe two or three years older than me, face down, being pinned to the floor with her arms held behind her back by one member of staff. Another sat on her feet and legs while she screamed, 'I don't want this, get off me. When I get up, you're both dead.'

I quickly got ushered along a corridor, away from the scene, and the head told me that was just someone who was having a bad day, nothing to worry about. Little did I know it would be an everyday occurrence.

I got to the head's office and she asked me to go in, then called in another member of staff; a short, round lady with very large beer-bottle glasses. She smiled and introduced herself as Edna, then they shut the door and showed me the uniform I had to wear. They said it was the smallest one they had. It consisted of a grey skirt, a green and white striped shirt, which sort of reminded me of the Aqua Fresh advert, and a green jumper and white socks. They told me to take my clothes off and change into it. They said they would turn around if I felt more comfortable. I looked at myself, looked at the clothes and thought, just do it quickly. My clothes were easy to take off, but the new uniform had a rigid feel to it. The head asked me if I needed help, which I agreed to, and then it was on. The green jumper sleeves were way below my hands and had to be rolled up at least four times, the shirt was just past my knees, and the skirt that was supposed to be just past my knees was just above my ankles; the white socks were a bit big but I liked the feel of them – I couldn't remember the last time I had new socks. The head and the lady looked down at me and the head said, 'Don't worry, you will grow into it.'

I got shown to a dormitory where I would have my own bed but sleep in a room full of other girls. There were 12 beds in total. I got told there were other dormitories up the corridor but this one was mine, and that it was called 'Night'. I later found out that the other dormitories were called 'Street' and 'New Wing'.

I tried to settle into the dormitory, but none of the other girls spoke to me; they just talked among themselves. It was my first day, so of course, no one was going to talk to me, I reasoned.

Every day after that was the same routine. We had house mums who were adults that looked after us. They used to wake us up in the morning and then we would get up and go down to the bathrooms, wash our faces and brush our teeth. After that, we would go back up to the dormitory and put our school uniform on, then line up to go down to breakfast, which was usually cereal and something on toast. I had marmalade on toast for the first time, and I loved it. Afterwards, we would line up to go to assembly. We would sing a song at the beginning, someone would tell a story or do a reading, and then we would have a piece of music. Assembly would always end with us all saying the Lord's Prayer in unison.

After that, we would head off to our different classes for the day, have lunch – lunch would be anything from fish, chips and peas, to bangers and mash – then at 3p.m., we would head back upstairs for social time, where the house mums would be waiting for us. We would take our uniforms off and put our own clothes on, then, after a while, line up for tea. Tea would always be something on toast, tinned tomatoes, beans, scrambled egg. I wasn't a fan of the tomatoes on toast – it used to make the toast soggy really quickly.

After tea, if you had been good, you went upstairs to the dormitory and watched TV or read books or sat and chatted in the TV room, then it was a shower and bed. If you were bad, you would go to detention after tea and either write lines or do times tables, then you would do have to do a job, either laying the chairs out for assembly the next day or laying the tables for breakfast the next morning, before having a shower and heading to bed.

The routine would have been the same every day, except that someone would always kick off at some point: they didn't want to get up, they didn't want breakfast, they didn't want to wear socks or they just felt like being defiant. Whatever the excuse was, it was always something, so there would be a scene and then they would get restrained. Occasionally, they would back down and we would go back to routine, but a lot of the time, I just carried on as normal because I knew it was going to happen at some point. I learnt later that children with special needs don't always see reason, and a lot of the time, when they want attention, they want it now, and there is no in-between. I was very scared because it was all new and so sudden, so I kept very quiet. People kicking off was different and I didn't like it and didn't understand it; the anger reminded me of home. I didn't miss being at home at all, I was happy for the break. Slowly, I got used to the teachers. I found I did really well in English and languages, but I was very poor in maths, geography and history. It had been a big change, but the people seemed nice and for now, I was happy.

CHAPTER FIFTEEN
Learning Routine

Age 13

I settled in eventually. There were lots of girls with severe problems, which were out of their control. One girl would beat her chest if she got angry, to the point where it would bruise; another girl would sit on the floor and pull her hair out; another would constantly bite parts of her body if she got nervous or upset. Others had less severe problems such as dyslexia, learning difficulties, or were just angry.

The first weeks were really good; I really enjoyed it. I was learning so much that I hadn't learned before, and being away from the violence was nice. There was routine and structure, and my days were filled with lots of different things. After lunch, we would hang out in the playground. At 3p.m., we would finish our lessons and head back upstairs to the dorm, where our house mums would be there to greet us. I don't know why, but I always liked teatime – it was usually something on toast, scrambled egg, tinned tomatoes or beans.

At 8p.m., it was lights out time. The house mums would say goodnight, make sure we were tucked in and then leave. They would swap over with the night staff, who would sit just outside the dorm all night until the house mums came back the next morning and then the day would start again.

Being a special needs school, people would kick off all the time for one reason or another; maybe they were having a bad day or they didn't want to learn. If the girls got aggressive or out of control, they would be restrained on the floor by up to three members of staff (as I saw on my first day). They would put the girl on the floor as quick as they could, put her arms up behind her back while another member of staff would hold their legs. They told us it was necessary because if you were out of control and going to disrupt others, certain measures had to be taken to protect you and everyone else.

Usually, one person kicking off would set another person off, so any learning or quiet time could be quickly ruined. Instead of studying, we would just watch someone face-down screaming the odds, their face so angry and disgruntled, with two or three members of staff red-faced, pinning them to the ground, waiting for them to calm down. Afterwards, they would take the girl off somewhere quiet and talk to her to find out what the problem was and get to the bottom of what started it all. After that, the girl would get detention for being disruptive. Detentions were their way of trying to teach us to talk about our problems rather than acting them out.

***

I was nervous when term ended and I had to go home and face things. I hadn't spoken to either Barbara or my dad throughout the first term, so I had been really excited to tell them about what I had learnt and seen at school, but when I got home, Dad beat the chattiness out of me because I had forgotten my place. I had forgotten I wasn't supposed to talk so much, especially when he was drunk. As I lay there, bloodied up again, Barbara stepped over me, sighed, and said, 'Will you ever learn?' Then, for the five weeks I was home, a bash here, a bash there, a slipper for good measure. If it wasn't Dad doing it, it was Barbara. It was hard going back to my old life. I felt like I was two different people and living two different ways – one at home and one at school.

I missed school so much. It was different this time; I wasn't sad, I was angry, angry with the school for putting me back here. I was happy at school; I was sore and miserable here. When it was time to go back, I couldn't wait for the clock to rush forward so I could be within the safe walls of school. As soon as I stepped through the school doors, all of my fear disappeared. I knew I didn't have to be the scared little mouse.

A few days back at school and a member of staff I liked asked me if I enjoyed the holidays. The rage just surfaced instantly. I felt like it was her fault, with her happy, chirpy voice, like she knew what was going to happen to me at home. Before I knew it, I had shouted, lost control, and pushed her with both my hands and all my might. This is what happens when you have had no kind of love or nurturing or even a simple hug. You kick off with pure unadulterated anger and hatred, like your body is exploding because you can't take it anymore. It was the first time I experienced being restrained. They held my hands up behind my back so tightly that I couldn't even move them. I screamed my heart out until my throat hurt, whilst they rocked me gently and said 'Shh'or 'Let it all out' softly in my ear.

I was so unused to this comfort. It really soothed my anger. I ended up a crying mess; that rocking and the soft words and the tight hold gave me a closeness I had never had before. It was amazing and addictive.

After that, my outbursts became a regular occurrence. All the rage I had been harbouring for Dad, I was able to offload at school. I would get restrained and scream my heart out and the anger would disappear. I would be able to speak about my anger afterwards, which I had never done before. But I would never breathe a word of what happened at home. I'd say that I was angry inside and I didn't know why. I would get a hug after, which was the best bit. It made me feel warm and fuzzy. I had not had that feeling before. I started to learn the rules and started to fit in. Routine was good for me; I knew where I had to be and when. I had one problem though; if I liked a class, I would excel in it, put a hundred per cent in –I did this with French, English, P.E –but if there was a subject I wasn't interested in, my mind would wander and I would fall far behind –this happened with maths, geography and history. It was like my brain would say, 'I'm bored now, it's too complicated' and I couldn't get it to work. I got told off many times for this.

A member of staff sat down with me one day and told me that I was 13 now and I didn't have to make a scene to get a cuddle, I could just ask for one. So I asked for one right there and then. She put her arms out and squeezed me ever so tightly, telling me there was always a cuddle waiting with her whenever I needed one. I was so happy that someone said I could have a cuddle whenever I wanted. I needed it, I liked it; no one had ever done that before.

After that, I calmed down and didn't have angry outbursts, and I asked for cuddles when I felt angry or sad. She didn't ask questions, she just gave me hugs, and I felt grown up now having this newfound knowledge that you could just ask for a cuddle.

There was a pay phone at school if you wanted to ring home or if your parents wanted to ring you. I never used it; I had no need. One day, during the second term, I got told I had a phone call.

I picked up the phone and said, 'Hello.' I could hear Barbara screaming in the background. Dad was slurring down the phone, saying that he was going to kill her then kill me, and he was going to post my body parts back to the school in little brown bags, and that I was a little piece of know-it-all shit, and that when I came home, he was going to bash me and all my new school friends to show us that we weren't as smart as we made out. I slammed the phone down, scared and angry. I knew how to ask for a hug but I didn't know how to stop this anger that was vibrating through my body; it was swirling round me so fast, I couldn't get a grip on it quick enough, and that's when it happened. In that moment, I picked up a chair and threw it across the room, followed by a plant. I saw my contorted face in the reflection of the window, so I picked up a table and threw it at the glass. The whole window smashed into a million pieces and the cold, dark air came flying in. People came from everywhere to see what had happened. In my head, I thought 'Run, go out the window', but before I had a chance to move, three members of staff slammed me to the ground. With all my might and the rage inside me, I managed to push them off so I could get to my knees, angrily spitting the words 'Get off me, don't come near me, I will hurt you, all of you.' They forcefully slammed me back down, but I was raging, determined to get free. I was like a wild animal, using everything I had to fight them off from the floor, getting my hand free and swinging out, kicking my legs, trying to bite whatever I could get to, wriggling to try and get free, bucking like a bronco to get them off, all the while screaming and shouting until I had nothing left; my steam had run out. I couldn't get them off me. I put my head down, my face in the carpet, panting and crying. I couldn't fight anymore, I was done.

The one member of staff who had said there was always a cuddle waiting for me had come down the backstairs. I looked over at her; she was standing there watching it all. She shook her head in disappointment. She walked over to me and said, 'I thought you were better than this, I obviously got you wrong. You don't want to be a better person, do you? My time will now be better spent with people who genuinely want to change for the better.' With that, she walked away. I lay there crying till one of the members of staff asked if I was going to fight anymore. I shook my head. They slowly got off me one at a time while I lay still, too tired to move. One of them sat me up. I could see red rings around my ankles and wrists where they had been holding me so tight and a friction burn on my arm from the carpet. A member of staff asked if I wanted to talk about it. I said, 'No.' In my head, I thought what's the point, nothing's going to change. Dad is going to kill me anyway.

***

When I got home for half-term, he didn't kill me; he just put me in hospital for two weeks. Barbara called an ambulance because I didn't wake up, and she thought he had killed me. Later, I found out they had told the paramedics that I had mental problems and went to a special school because of that. They also said I had a sugar addiction that made me go crazy and I had climbed the kitchen cupboards looking for the sugar and the cupboards had come away from the wall, crashing down on me – that's how they explained the injuries.

Dad had a smart mouth when he was drunk. He would threaten and say all kinds of things. He would also have this unstoppable rage that would come out of nowhere; you either shut your mouth or you paid the price, but even when you were quiet, you weren't safe. He was like a ticking time bomb. He knew he could hurt me because I wouldn't fight back. When I got home that day from school, he was shouting things about me being a smart ass now and how I thought I was better than him and Barbara because I had a new school and friends. He just kept hitting me with his fists over and over, until I fell on the floor. He then repeatedly punched me until it all went black. I never went near the kitchen cupboards. I didn't have mental problems but that's what he told the paramedics when they turned up at our house.

I lay in the hospital and could only slightly open one eye, the other eye was sealed shut. I hurt all over. I didn't even know what my injuries were, but it was bad. Barbara was the first person I saw. She stood over me and said, 'Thank God, I thought you were dead. Your Dad is so angry, he has told me to tell you to keep your mouth shut or...' Tears stopped her finishing her sentence, until she muttered, 'You know as well as I do what will happen. Just be a good girl.' I turned my head away from her and shut my eye. 'A thank you would be nice. You would have been dead if it wasn't for me,' Barbara said.

The next thing I remember was being woken by a lady calling my name. I opened my eye as best as I could. She was wearing a suit. She asked if I was comfortable and whether I needed anything. It was general chit-chat. I didn't answer; I just listened. She then explained what Barbara and Dad had said had happened and asked me whether that was right. I nodded my head but my neck gave me such a sharp pain, I cried out. She asked if I needed a nurse and I said, 'No,' and decided not to move my neck anymore.

She then tried to befriend me and told me she was on my side, and if I had anything to say, now was the time to say something. She spoke about abuse in the home and how children were too scared to talk and that she was a voice for them. She told me I had to speak up if there was any wrongdoing. I didn't say anything; I knew full well I wasn't uttering a word about what had happened. I was frustrated because I wanted to tell her the truth. I wanted to explain everything right from the beginning until now, but I daren't because I knew what he would do to me and I couldn't take that risk.

She asked me if Dad beat me, if Barbara beat me, if any people came to the house other than those two who had hurt me. I said 'No' to each question. Unable to get anything from me, she left. I didn't speak up because I knew that if I did, it would be a lot worse, and I was terrified at the thought of that.

I would like to say the two weeks in hospital were good but they weren't. I was very uncomfortable a lot of the time, I was often in pain, I needed medication, and I slept a lot. Eventually, after the two weeks were up, I was well enough to go home. A different lady came to the ward and said she was taking me home. When we got to the house, Barbara opened the door, and we went inside and all sat down on the sofa. Dad sat next to me and got me around the neck, pulling me into him, pretending to be all playful, saying, 'You gave us a scare there, kid.' I winced in pain as my neck still hurt a lot. The lady asked him to be gentle with me as I'd had severe injuries and I still needed to heal. With that, he let go of me and ruffled my hair instead. He carried on his act and said, 'We just missed her a lot, that's all.'

The lady didn't seem convinced and said, 'Because of her injuries, your family will now be monitored. We know it was a normal household accident but we can never be too careful. Domestic abuse happens daily.' Dad started laughing, but the lady said, 'Domestic abuse is no laughing matter.'

Dad stood with his hands on his hips and said to her, 'Do we look like a family who would beat up their kid? Does she look like she gets smacked? No, we take care of her and give her what she needs.'

The lady butted in, 'It doesn't matter what you look like. Domestic abuse can happen in all sorts of different families, it's not just one stereotype.'

With that, Dad sat down.

She opened a black folder and started to list dates and times she would drop in and see us. Dad told her that I was at boarding school because I had special needs and that I only came home for the holidays. She said that was fine, she still wanted to observe my home life with or without me being there. She scrawled writing down in the file. She said goodbye to me. I never saw her again.

CHAPTER SIXTEEN
Emma

Age 13

I was just about healed by the time the five weeks were up. The bruises were faint marks, and I was still a bit sore in places, but I wanted to be back at school, away from the madness.

Back at school, I made a friend. Her name was Emma. She had long, blonde hair and was quiet and shy. She said she was at the school because she was dyslexic. She asked why I was at the school. I answered that I was not messed up, I just got messed up.

Her bed was opposite mine in the dormitory. I would wake early, but she would already be awake. She had two soft toys at the end of her bed; one large, fluffy, white cat and a large, brown dog. Emma used to pick them up and make them dance together to make me laugh. We couldn't talk because of the risk of waking everyone else, so she entertained us most mornings, and I enjoyed every minute of it.

Over time, we became best friends. I liked Emma; she didn't ask questions about my new bruises, fresh marks or home life. If the staff asked about my bruises or marks, I would tell them that I had been sleepwalking or that I had fallen over. Emma just wanted to be friends and laugh with me. I enjoyed laughing, laughing was a new thing.

I felt like she was everything I could want in a friend. We would have our lessons together and hang out in our social time, we spoke about how we both loved cats, but we also loved all animals and our dream job would be to care for animals.

Emma gave me her phone number in case I ever wanted to talk to her in the school holidays. She proudly wrote her phone number in the front cover of my favourite book. Emma didn't have my phone number because I didn't know it, but she said that was fine; once I had called her, she could dial 1471 and find out my number. So I said I would call.

The Christmas holiday was fast approaching again and our friendship would have to come to a halt for now. When it was time to go our separate ways to go home, we had a long hug and said our goodbyes.

During the school holiday, I wasn't allowed to talk for very long, but Barbara said I could have 20 minutes talking to Emma, and she timed it. It was nice to have someone to talk to and not be alone in holiday time. The 20 minutes flew by and Emma said she would dial 1471 after the call and keep my number safe. Then, with the time up, we said our goodbyes.

The phone bill came in one day and Dad came into my room in the early hours of the morning while I was asleep. He was his usual drunk self. There was a rocking chair in my room and I woke to him rocking backwards and forwards in it, saying *nee naw, nee naw* every time he went back and forward. I sat up in bed and could see he had a piece of paper in his hand. Then he stopped rocking.

He said someone was in trouble for using the phone to call their cranky school mates. I sat motionless, staring at him. I knew something was going to happen but I didn't know what.

He flew at me. I quickly lay down and pulled the covers over my head, and he punched the cover on top of my head continuously. I held on to the bedclothes as tight as I could, like my life depended on it. Then he stopped. There was silence, then he made a loud kissing noise on top of my head and said, 'See you in the morning, kid.' I heard my door shut. I didn't move and I didn't release the cover.

The next morning, there was no way I was going downstairs. I knew what was in store for me and I thought if I stayed out of the way, there might be a chance it would all just go away.

Barbara shouted upstairs for me to come down. I didn't have a choice; I had to go. I walked slowly downstairs and could feel the fear in my tummy going around like a washing machine on spin cycle. I didn't know if Dad was in, but for some reason, I could sense that he was.

I got to the bottom tread, took a deep breath and stood in the living room doorway. Barbara was standing with her arms crossed. Dad was in his chair, smoking and watching TV.

Barbara said, 'Your Dad wants to talk to you. Do as you're told and don't piss him off.' She then left and walked into the kitchen.

Dad left me standing there for what seemed like forever until his programme finished. It was like I was on death row, waiting for the almighty blow. My tummy hurt now because I was so nervous.

When his programme finished, he reached for the remote and turned the TV off. He walked over to me slowly and said quietly, 'So you want to use the phone like a big girl, you want to phone your nutty friends like a big girl. I suppose you tell your nutty friends what goes on here like a big girl. Am I right?'

I was scared, so I looked down at my feet. I was already starting to cry and nothing had even happened yet. He repeated, with his face close to mine, 'Do you tell your nutty friends what happens here?'

I pulled away from him and shook my head. Then he grabbed me by the throat and slammed my head up against the wall behind me, shouting in my face, 'Don't lie to me.'

He grabbed the phone receiver and hit me in the face with it, repeating, 'You don't use the phone. The phone is not for you. You don't call anyone.'

Every time he said a word, he would hit me with the phone: 'You – *hit* – don't – *hit* – use – *hit* –the – *hit* –phone.'

It hurt so much, but I couldn't scream with pain because his grip around my throat was so tight. He squeezed tighter every time he hit me.

I could feel my eyes bulging, ready to pop out of my head. I needed to breathe, I needed air. I thought I was going to die.

One final blow and he was done. He let go of me and said, 'Let's hope you have learned your lesson.'

I fell to the floor on my stomach, coughing and trying to get as much air as I could. My chest hurt from lack of air, and I felt like I was going to die. I kept sucking up the air really fast like I had never breathed before, deep breaths in and out, panting while I gently held my throat. When I finally got some of my breath back, I started to cry, which made it hard to breathe again.

Dad stood over me and shouted, 'You're not a baby, are you?' I put my hand up to somehow stop what he was going to do. 'Babies cry,' he said. 'Keep crying and I'll give you something to cry for.' He then kicked me in the stomach with an almighty blow and said, 'Get upstairs.' I lay there, holding my stomach, rolling in pain. He shouted again, 'Get upstairs.' Somehow, I scrambled off the floor, but fell back down. He grabbed me by my clothes and dragged me to the bottom of the stairs and then walked away. I think I managed to block out the pain with just fear alone. I crawled halfway up the stairs but I couldn't go any further – I had to rest. I eventually got to my room and lay on the bedroom floor. Barbara came upstairs with a washing basket, stuck her head in my door and said, 'I told you not to piss him off.'

I lay there for however long it took, until it didn't hurt to get up. I felt sick and dizzy. My face felt like a hundred candles had burnt it. When Barbara had gone back downstairs, I went to the bathroom to check the damage. That side of my face had instantly started to swell. I couldn't open my right eye and all around it had started to blacken. My top and bottom lip on one side were very swollen and there was a cut on my bottom lip. I tried to put water on my face to calm the heat down but it hurt too much. I saw a scrunched-up flannel on the side of the bath, rinsed it out, ran it under the cold water and held it on the burning part of my face. It stung, but the cold against the heat felt like some sort of release. I went back to my bedroom and sat on the floor. I could feel a headache coming. I didn't want to be here. I wanted to be at school.

A couple of days later, I could just about open my eye. It was red and bloodshot all over the eyeball. My eye was all shiny and it hurt like hell. Barbara had to go to town and didn't want to leave me at home, which usually meant she needed help with the shopping bags, so we left the house. She went around the market, with me following behind like I normally did, carrying bags and waiting while she shopped.

Barbara saw someone she knew that she hadn't seen in a while, and they started chatting. I had my back to them while they were talking; I was watching a man playing a musical instrument and loved the way it sounded. The music took me to a faraway place. I didn't know where, but it wasn't here.

The lady must have asked about me and Barbara barked, 'Oi you, come over here.'

The lady noticed my eye. She was shocked and laughed half-heartedly, asking, 'What happened to her, have you been beating her?'

Barbara got really defensive and said, 'No, she has mental problems and is really clumsy, she ran into a door.' She then started shouting at the lady, 'You want to be careful saying things like that, they can get you in a lot of trouble.' She grabbed me and bolted off, literally dragged me to the taxi rank, opened the door of a taxi, shouting at me to get in, then threw herself in the passenger seat next to the driver, roaring our address at him.

When we got home, she picked up the phone, called the pub and asked the barman for Dad. She shouted down the phone at Dad, telling him what happened, and said she was not taking me with her anymore; I would have to stay at the pub with him from now on when she went into town. She slammed the phone down and shouted in my face, 'You're nothing but trouble, you are.' She shoved me from behind and said, 'Get upstairs, I don't even want to look at you, you're disgusting.'

I went to my room as usual. I wanted to scream and shout and run away, be by myself. Surely, nothing could be worse than this. I hated my life. I had nothing to live for. No one loved me. I was just a thing, a thing that everyone had to take care of. I thought again about running away, but reasoned they would only find me and hurt me for doing it. I sat on the floor at the foot of the bed. I was angry that nobody loved me, I didn't understand why. What did I do to be so unlovable?

A few hours later, Barbara came upstairs, opened my door and said, 'Your Dad's paralytic at the pub again, go and get him.'

I picked myself up off the floor, went out of the front door into the dark. A couple of times on the long walk into town, I thought of diverting off and going somewhere else, but I had nowhere to go. So I kept going till I got to the pub.

Chapter Seventeen
Messing Around

Age 13

The Christmas holidays were finally over; the taxi was coming to pick me up as usual to take me back to school. I was so excited; it was time to be free of here and the nasties that went with it. My eye was semi back to normal – there was still some bruising but it didn't look as bad. Nobody at school asked much about my bruises, and when they did, they believed the sleepwalking story, so I didn't care much about what it looked like, I just wanted to be back. I heard the taxi *beep* while I was sitting on the bed waiting, with my bag packed. I grabbed my bag and shot down the stairs two at a time. I could hardly contain my happiness.

At the bottom, I came to a halt. Dad was standing in front of the closed front door. I stood holding my bag tightly, trying to calm my breathing. He leant into me, pointing his finger in my face and said, 'You say anything to those teachers of yours or your dotty friends and I'll have you when you come back, you hear me?' I nodded. He put his fist on my chin and gave it a push so my head moved. 'Now fuck off,' he said, and opened the front door.

The sun was shining brightly and as soon as I was outside the door, my spirits lifted. I ran to the taxi as fast as my little legs would take me. I opened the door, Emma was inside.

I was shocked but so happy. Emma was in the taxi, I couldn't believe it, I laughed. Emma laughed too and said in a mocking voice, 'I know where you live now.'

When I had put my seat belt on, the taxi driver turned around and said that from now on he was going to pick us both up as we lived close to each other; she was in the next town but that was hardly anything in a car. He said he would drop us back together every half-term. He also said the lady sitting next to him was called Cheryl and she was the escort in case we kicked off or basically tried to kill him while he was driving. Cheryl gave us a friendly smile then a childlike wave and asked us if we were going to give her any trouble. Together, in sync, we both said 'no', then looked at each other and laughed at how in tune we were. We gripped each other's hands and held on tight. We were both so happy we were together, me more so I think, because of all that had happened in the holidays. With Emma, I didn't feel alone.

That day, on the way to school, we got stuck in a two-hour traffic jam and it was the best traffic jam I had ever been in. Emma had a bag of sweets that she shared around. Cheryl put the radio on and we all sang loudly to the songs and imitated the instruments and acted the dance moves. As the car crawled along at a snail's pace, Emma waved at people through the window and we laughed hysterically when people waved back. We talked about school and wondered what the teachers and the other children had been up to. Emma told me what she had done in the holidays, ending that towards the end, she had got a bit bored and wanted to go back to school. She asked what I had done. 'Nothing much, I was just bored all the time,' I lied.

***

We had been at school for a week and Emma and I were put in detention for messing around in class together. We had to do times tables and I hated numbers, I didn't understand them, so whenever the teacher left the room for a minute, Emma and I would throw a pen or bits of paper with notes on to each other.

Detention was finally over and we got the job of laying the tables for breakfast the next morning. In the dining room, we were playing around, but at the same time, doing what we were supposed to. Emma did the crockery, I did the cutlery.

I was at the far end of the room and Emma was at the other. I had a teaspoon in my hand and I shouted to Emma, 'I bet I can hit you on the head from all the way over here.'

'Ha, I bet you can't,' Emma said.

'Are you going to move if I throw it?'

'Not a chance,' Emma said. 'I dare you!'

The teaspoon flew through the air heading for Emma. She watched it as it came towards her, both of us transfixed.

The teaspoon hit her square between the eyes, and she fell back and slid down the wall behind her. I stood there in shock for what felt like five minutes. Emma was out of view behind the big dining tables. Suddenly, she jumped up and started laughing like a hyena, saying, 'I'm OK,' holding the teaspoon like a trophy.

Instant relief came over my whole body. I weaved through the tables and ran over to her, laughing, and I hugged her and said I was sorry. She hugged me back and tapped me on the head with the teaspoon and said, 'It was OK.'

We were laughing and talking, shocked at how the teaspoon had hit her so accurately. We started re-enacting the whole thing, dancing around. We thought it was hilarious and completely forgot the time. A teacher came in and saw that the tables hadn't been laid, and that we had been messing about. We got another detention for the next day.

CHAPTER EIGHTEEN
Cross Country

Age 13

We had plenty of opportunities at school to keep us active and fit – we had gym equipment, roller blades, and we used to play rounders. I always loved sports day. I was pretty good; cross country and swimming were my favourites. I used to love being under the water, swimming by myself. I liked the mumbly silence – it made me feel alive – and those moments of quiet were nice. I was a good swimmer. I liked the competitive racing; swimming hard and fast was another way of me channelling my anger. I enjoyed the achievement of getting to the end of the length, somersaulting under the water, kicking off the edge and blasting my way back, powering my arms and legs and giving it everything I had, not knowing how far people were behind me.

Cross country was another release for me. We used to run for miles over rough ground with a start and finish point and checkpoints along the way. Some girls weren't mentally or physically able to do it, so they either sat out or walked it. I would stand at the start, waiting for the word 'go', my feet itching to blast away from my body. A teacher had a stopwatch round her neck and I would watch intently for her to push the two buttons on the watch and shout, 'Go!' I would put everything into those first paces; I needed to get as far in front as possible as fast as possible. I would let my feet do the hard work and did everything I could with the rest of my body to keep my stamina – breathing in through the nose, out through the mouth.

Occasionally, I would look behind me until no one was in sight. For a while, I was free, nothing could hurt me mentally or physically, though the adrenaline made me think of home. I had only felt this sort of adrenaline when I was there, but at school, I was in control of it. I ran from my thoughts. I just kept running harder and faster, trying to distance myself from the world. Teachers clapped me at every checkpoint, which just pushed me to run faster. I got to the finish and laid on the floor, puffing and panting, my heart feeling like it was going to jump out of my chest and take a rest beside me. Breathing was hard; there was a cold sharp pain in my chest and side. It hurt but it was worth it. I made it, I won. It felt great.

CHAPTER NINETEEN
Fifty Red Roses

Age 13

Home for the half-term holiday again.

I didn't know much about anything. Neither Barbara nor my dad taught me any home, living or life skills, so I only knew the basics and what I learned at school. But I did know one thing, and that's that we were poor, and we were only poor because Dad used to drink all the money. Some weeks, we would eat; other weeks, we would only eat sugar sandwiches, because that's all we could afford: bread, butter and sugar. Barbara would butter the bread and sprinkle sugar on it, add another slice on top and there you had it – breakfast, lunch and dinner. She fed me this and repeatedly told social services that I had a sugar problem.

We would constantly run out of gas and electricity, and sometimes, Barbara would go next door and the neighbours would let her use their cooker or feel sorry for us and give us some handouts.

Dad and Barbara wouldn't go without cigarettes though. They would go to the local shop and the shop would give them cigarettes if they paid for them when their next money came in.

Dad would still go down the pub and his pub friends would buy him beers, even though the reason we had no money was because of his drinking.

When Dad was drunk, he would buy things he couldn't afford, which would be most of the time.

The first time the debt collector came round, we were sitting eating our dinner on our laps, watching TV. We had a dining table but it was so covered in junk, it never got used, unless Barbara was having one of her spur of the moment spring cleans, which was hardly ever.

There was a loud bang on the door and a voice shouted, 'Debt collector.' Dad shot out of his chair as fast as he could and turned off the TV and the lights. He ushered Barbara into the kitchen and grabbed me in a head lock, telling me to shut my mouth and not say a word. He was sitting behind me on the kitchen floor, his hairy forearm tightly around my neck. I knew it was a warning, so I sat as still as I could.

There was loud banging on the door again. It was deathly silent. I was scared because I didn't know what was going on. Another bang on the door came. It made me jump and this time and I squeaked. Because of that, Dad tightened his grip and with the other hand, slapped my face hard. He whispered viciously into my ear, 'Cry and I'll give you something to cry for.'

It was so hard not to cry, but I couldn't risk it because of what he would do to me. I was trying to hold it in as much as I could, but what made it worse was the hot sting I could feel humming on the skin of my face, the tears willing themselves at the back of my eyes, the adrenaline inside taunting me to cry.

The lady at the door opened our letterbox and Dad's grip on me tightened even more, making it difficult for me to breathe. She shouted through the letterbox, 'Open the door, I know you're in there.'

About a minute passed, although it felt longer. She shut the letterbox and we heard footsteps walking away. Dad let go of me. I put my hands on the floor, grateful to be released, taking massive gulps of air. My tears let themselves drop uninvited. Dad went to the curtains; he must have seen her leave because he put the lights back on and turned on the TV, lit a cigarette and sat in his chair, flicking the remote for something to watch. I picked myself up and ran straight to my room.

The lady came back a couple of days later and Dad handed her some money. She said he was lucky she didn't have to bring reinforcements. I didn't know what that meant at the time; I just peered around the kitchen door and watched. It was one of the only times I'd seen my dad look sheepish, like he was uncomfortable with the situation. Nothing changed after that though; he still did the same, drank the money away, still made us poor.

The next week was Barbara's 50th birthday. As usual, Dad was at the pub. A man knocked at the door around lunchtime and Barbara opened it to 50 red roses. Dad had impulse spent again. She cried because, to her, it was a sign he loved her.

She handed me roses after roses to take into the kitchen. She used all the vases we had, then saucepans, glasses, bowls, anything she could find until the last rose was finally in water. Our kitchen looked like a small garden centre, a mass of roses dotted all over the place.

Barbara sat on a chair in the kitchen, lit up a cigarette and started to cry, saying that he could never do anything properly, he always had to go over the top and ruin everything. She wasn't talking to me directly but to herself. I just stood there listening. I had no compassion for her and I didn't want to comfort her so I just watched her ramble on. She hated this life, but she had nothing else. Even when something good happened, you could trust her to see something bad. She couldn't just be happy and be done with it.

She went into the living room and phoned Anne, and started to tell her what had happened. I put the TV on and sat on the floor to watch it.

Later, Dad came home, completely off his face. He was very loving to Barbara, telling her he loved her, while he slurred and hung all over her. They went into the kitchen and he was very proud of himself for the roses, and started telling Barbara that he was the best husband in the world and that no other husband would give her all those roses, and didn't she think they were brilliant. He told her that she probably thought he had forgotten her birthday but he hadn't.

Barbara started to cry. I got up from watching the TV and stood in the kitchen doorway. She got angry and told him that every time he does something bad, he tries to make amends by doing something over the top, stupid, and this was ridiculous because she had nowhere to put all the roses, and he could have done something small and she would have liked it, rather than having too many poxy flowers. She shouted, 'They are in saucepans, for Christ's sake.'

He was silent for a minute while he stared at her, then he shouted, 'You ungrateful bitch.' He grabbed her and pushed her up against the cooker, holding her by the throat and choking her. She struggled to breathe, and tried to grab at his arm to stop him.

I hated what I was watching so I shouted, 'Stop.'

He turned his head around and looked at me, and in a calm, controlled voice, said, 'You shut your mouth or you're next.'

Out of nowhere, Barbara got the strength she needed to free herself from his grip. Gulping big gasps of air, she grabbed him by his hair. I could see by her face, she was fuming, she was at breaking point. She towered above him, which made him look tiny. She got his head and smashed it into the fridge door. I didn't know what to do; this had been the first time I had seen her fight back. Her extremely large frame and the momentary strength made him unable to move. He hit the fridge with an almighty blow. She pulled his head back like she was going to do it again. He was powerless to move, and she leaned into his face and screamed, 'You are not going to do this to me anymore.' She stared at him, shaking, while holding his head in her hand, her whole body enraged. She let out an almighty scream, right in his face, and then just let go of him, letting him drop to the floor, saying, 'You're not worth it.'

She leant over the sink, her head in her arms, and started crying. With her size and the little bit of strength she had for that moment, she could have done him some serious damage, even killed him and ended it all for all of us. But she didn't, she didn't have it in her.

I stood there for five minutes, unsure what to do. She was still crying, he was still lying on the floor, and I was stuck to the spot. I couldn't help anyone. I had never been in this situation before. I was scared and I didn't know what I was supposed to do.

Moments later, he got up from the floor and ripped Barbara away from the sink and threw her to the ground, kicking and punching her into the floor while she covered her face. I couldn't move. It had all happened so quickly. He shouted while he kicked and punched, 'You ever fucking do that to me again and I will fucking kill you, do you hear me? I will kill you.'

Blow after blow, he hit her, then when he thought she had had enough, he looked up and stopped and stared at me. I stepped back with my hand outstretched saying, 'No, no, please, no.'

He was there in my face. He grabbed me with one hand and pushed me up against the door with the other. He said, 'My own flesh and blood, and you just stood there and watched! You did nothing, nothing to help me. My own daughter! You deserve everything you get,' he roared, as he lifted his fist high in the air. He was too close. His nose now touched the end of mine. 'Fuck you, mini me,' he shouted, as he brought his fist down hard on my nose and face. I was flung to the floor; the pain was unbearable. I could see white dots floating.

I screamed in pain, my hand shot up to my face. He grabbed my hand away and smashed my face twice more with his fist. I was shaking and crying. He kept hitting me, and I kept trying to hold my face until I just lay there, unable to protect myself because I was too dazed. My head was spinning. He walked away. My face hurt so much, my head was throbbing, and I was so scared. I lay on the floor, looking through the tear glasses I was now wearing, and watched my blood drip from my face and form a puddle in front of me. I looked further and saw Barbara lying motionless, on the bloody floor. I shut my eyes and felt the pumping sensation in my face, along with the constant sharp shots of pain. I was still shaking, I couldn't calm down enough to stop it, and it made my face hurt more.

I lay there all night until morning. I didn't want to get up for fear of something else happening. I didn't sleep; I hurt too much for that. In the morning, Barbara eventually moved and sat up, shuffling herself until her back was against the fridge. She had huge cut marks on her mouth, above her eye, under her eyes and on her hands. One of her eyes was completely bloody. There were blood stains coming from her nostrils. Her face was a mess. She tipped her head back and rested it on the fridge. With the back of her hand on her head, she panted like she was still winded. I sat up too, relieved that she was still alive.

We heard the front door shut as Dad decided to leave rather than face up to what he had done. Barbara told me to go upstairs and clean myself up. I got to my feet shakily, light-headed and wounded. I looked at her; I wanted to ask her if she needed help. She looked at me and said, 'Just go.'

Upstairs, I put my hands on the sink, lifted my head and looked in the mirror. I had a big, thick, deep cut across the bridge of my nose. It had stopped bleeding but was crusty with dried blood, and I could see fresh blood waiting to fall if it was disturbed. The stream of blood from my nostrils to my top lip had left two clearly-defined red lines. I had a blood-stained chin where the blood had fallen from my nose and settled there. The top of my nose was fat and swollen and my face was blotchy from all the tears. All around my eyes and the top of my nose was very dark and starting to bruise, and there were bits of smeared blood on my cheeks. I didn't even recognise it was me. I laughed at myself in the mirror. All this because of 50 red roses. Happy Birthday Barbara.

CHAPTER TWENTY
The Gas Fire

Age 14

I had so many late nights-early mornings of being forced to leave my bed and come downstairs to be a puppet for Dad and his newfound pub friends. The gas fire had been a godsend for all that unwanted food, which had been rammed in my face to eat in the early hours.

However, nothing lasts forever. Winter came, which meant it was time for the fire to come on. I was sitting on the sofa, reading a book, while Barbara and Dad watched TV. Barbara got up and went over to the fire, held down the knob and turned it. The fire made a ticking sound then all it had to do was light, but it didn't. She turned the knob back and then forward. Again, the ticking sound but no fire up. She turned it off and Dad got up to have a go. I was sitting there watching, willing the fire to light with all my heart, but it didn't. Barbara went into the kitchen and Dad was looking at the fire, trying to find the problem. Unable to, he sat back down. I was relieved: *that's it, it's broken so that's the end of it and I'm home free.* How wrong I was.

Four days later, a man in a blue boiler suit turned up at our door. Barbara shouted to Dad, 'It's the gas man.'

Dad told me to sit on the sofa and stay out of the man's way. I gingerly sat. Dad turned the knob and showed the man the problem. The gas man put a huge bag on the floor, took out a screwdriver and started unscrewing the front of the fire. Panic raced around my body and my hands were sweaty. I needed to run but there was nowhere to run to. Instead, I sat transfixed, waiting for the inevitable. It was just a ticking time bomb, the seconds counting down.

The man took the front of the fire off and in an instant, all this mouldy food cane tumbling down onto the floor. We all sat there staring at it for a couple of seconds. Then they all looked at me, Dad stared at me like he was going to explode and snarled at me to get upstairs. I kept staring at the mouldy food; there was so much of it, I didn't realise there was so much. Dad shouted louder at me, 'You heard me, get upstairs, now!' The severity of his voice brought me to my senses, and I belted it upstairs.

In my room, I paced up and down, I knew I was in trouble and I knew it was bad, no point hiding, no point trying to explain. It was a waiting game and not a very comfortable one.

I heard the gas man leave and Barbara and Dad talking, then shouting. I knew I was next. I thought maybe because Dad wasn't drunk, if I tried to, I could reason with him and explain.

I heard him coming up the stairs so I prepared myself. I stood in the middle of my room with my hands clasped in front of me, ready to state my case. He pushed open the door.

I started to say, 'I just want...' but I didn't get the chance.

He came at me and smashed a raw egg on my face, then hit me in my stomach and shouted, 'You don't want my food?' and then threw another raw egg at me, which smashed completely into my mouth. He shouted, 'You don't want to eat what's good for you?' before he punched me in my stomach and I keeled over.

I lay in a ball on the floor, holding my stomach with both hands while trying to spit the egg from my mouth, crunching it as I spit. The first egg was all in my eyes and hair, making it difficult to see. He grabbed the back of my neck and dragged me out of my bedroom, standing at the top of the stairs. He then lifted me off the ground with both hands, held me up and threw me down the stairs, shouting, 'Down you go.'

The treads gave me sharp, vicious blows as I fell. I lay at the bottom, winded and groaning as every part of my body hurt. I felt him coming down the stairs. I tried to get the stamina to crawl away but my body defeated me. Too hurt to move, I couldn't escape.

He stood in front of me and delivered a hard kick to my stomach. The blow forced my body against the front door. He grabbed me by my hair and dragged me into the living room. The fire had gone but the mouldy food was still there, a grey mass of sludge. He dropped me next to the awful food pile, held my head next to it and said, 'You're hungry now aren't you, you little bitch?' as he smeared the mouldy food all over my face. It was cold and stank. I tried to move my head away, but he started shoving it in my mouth. With all the energy I had left, I spat the food out, trying desperately not to breathe in. The smell was repulsive and the taste made me heave. Angrily, he tried to shove more of the food in my mouth but I kept my mouth shut as tightly as possible. He punched me in the face and banged my head on the floor. I opened my mouth as I wailed in pain, giving him the opportunity to stuff the mouldy food in my mouth. A repulsive taste hit the back of my throat, a vile death smell travelled up the back of my nostrils; my mouth was now filled with my clever mistake.

He rubbed my face in it with his heavy palm and then stood on my face with his foot and twisted it, like he was putting out a cigarette with his shoe. He spat on me, stood over me and told me I was as ungrateful as Barbara.

I lay there defeated, unable to move; I threw up on myself several times and passed out.

Later, when I opened my eyes, he had gone. I still couldn't move; my body hurt way too much, like it had given up. I tried but it wasn't happening. I saw a figure standing in the kitchen doorway; it was Barbara. She came over and picked me up. She had never picked me up before. She carried me into the garden and laid me on the grass. I looked up at her; she turned the hose on and soaked me. The water was freezing cold but my body was stiff. I felt winded and in shock from the cold spray. She turned off the hose, still not speaking, picked me up, took me upstairs and threw me onto my bed. Wet clothes and all. Then she shut the door and went downstairs.

WHAT NOBODY KNEW

Mrs believes child has built a wall around herself and no-one ever gets to see the true child Mrs describes child's personality as a complete facade. Underneath it all is a very sensitive girl but she keeps all her feelings hidden.

Child attended the Child and Family Clinic before going away to school. They felt she may have been sexually abused as her behaviour was indicating this. However, there has been no disclosure from child or any proof. For the first three years of her life she lived with her natural mother who passed her around from pillar to post and left her with anyone who would have her. When child went to live with her dad and step-mum she did not even know what a cuddle was.

Child very healthy physically but not emotionally. From the age of four she had a stomach complaint and projectile vomiting. She saw Dr. who did not at the time make a diagnosis. Four years later, at a school meeting, it came out that Dr. thought child had been anorexic. Mr. and Mrs. had always had trouble feeding child (she wouldn't eat and would hide the food everywhere) but they were not aware of the anorexia. Child eats now and this is no longer a problem. She is small in height and build but then so is her father.

Child has slight mood swings but these are not bad. As a small child (4 - 5 years old) she wanted to kill herself and would often talk of this. This lasted 6-9 months and she does not talk of this now.

Child attended JMI School (Mainstream) from the age of 4 to 9. She then spent one term at another School but the teachers could not

THE GAS FIRE

handle her behaviour so she left. She then went to another school with a Special Needs Unit between the ages of 9 -11 and she got on well there. At 11 she went to Greenwood School which is a school for girls with emotional and behavioural difficulties.

Child is doing well academically at this school. She likes debating in history and religion and is good at French and computer studies. She loves sport, especially swimming, and is a good all-round sportswoman. She has no problems with reading and writing.

Depending on the child, Greenwood School structures their pupils towards either G.C.S.E's or N.V.Q'S. It is still unclear which way child will go – it could be either way.

Child has experienced a separation from her birth mother. Her mother told child she was going shopping and never came back. At first child would cry when she went shopping with Mr. and Mrs. child believed she was looking for her mother in the shops. This stopped after six to seven months. child has asked questions about her mother and Mr. and Mrs. answer these questions as best as they can. Mrs. feels that child is very bitter about her mother.

Mr. sleeps during the day (as he works at nights) so is unable to help. Mrs. has health problems and trouble with mobility. She stopped work with depression and anxiety seven years ago. Mrs.is unable to do things with child i.e. take her out to various places, swimming etc. and cannot send her off alone as she is too vulnerable. Child copes fairly well with this but Mrs. feels she does miss out.

D.R.I
DETAIL RECORD

Client Name: *Child*   Tel. No:

child attends ▓▓▓▓▓▓ residential school for girls with emotional & educational difficulties. ▓▓▓▓▓▓ attends regular meetings & discussions at the school. child lives with her natural father and stepmother. ▓▓▓▓▓▓ thinks that she is the only child at home. When she goes home at weekends there is domestic violence & she is witnessing her father beating her mother. Father is an alcoholic. child has been saying to school staff that she has been cleaning up her father's vomit & the last time she was at home (about a weeks ago) her father hit her. Also telling staff that when she is at home she doesn't go out or have any friends as she needs to protect her mother from her father. child is stressed & anxious at school & when any other pupils shout it reminds her of her dad's screaming. ▓▓▓▓▓ & school are concerned that when school breaks up child will be at home for 6 weeks in this situation. ▓▓▓▓▓▓▓▓

▓▓▓▓▓▓▓▓▓▓▓▓▓▓▓▓▓▓▓▓▓▓▓▓▓▓▓▓▓▓

▓▓▓▓▓▓▓▓▓▓▓▓▓▓▓▓▓▓▓▓▓▓▓▓▓▓▓▓▓▓

Also says he is concerned about child going home at the weekend.

CHAPTER TWENTY-ONE
Divorce

Age 15

I was 15 when one of the teachers came to me, sat me down and explained a phone call had come through, telling them my parents were getting divorced. The teacher had been told so she could break the news to me and be there to give me support. I wasn't shocked; I didn't really care. Since the battering that put me in hospital, I had learnt not to care about anything; it made no difference to me what either of them did. The teacher explained that because it was a special circumstance, I was to go home for a week. My dad was moving out in a few days, and Barbara and Dad would sit down with me and explain what was going on when I got there. She told me that I would come back to school the week after, once I had understood everything. I was to get a bag together and my taxi would pick me up the next day.

The next day arrived and I hauled my bag in the taxi. I hated going home. The two hours in the car were nice and silent, sort of like the calm before the storm.

When I got home, Dad was coming down the stairs with suitcases and bags. I headed into the living room, immediately noticing there was something different about Barbara. She was bold, her head was held high, and her shoulders were back like she didn't care. Dad put his bags on the path outside the front door and went back for more. Barbara was acting like she had slayed the dragon.

'I told him enough was enough,' she said out loud, wobbling her head in agreement with herself. 'Did he listen though? No, he did not. I told him this day would come but he just carried on. Today is my day, my day.'

Dad stood in the doorway. He looked like a little boy who had just been told off. He handed Barbara his key and said he had got all his stuff, and just stood there with puppy eyes, looking at her. She said goodbye abruptly and held her arm up high, pointing to the front door. He slowly walked to the door, a taxi beeped outside; he picked up his bags and stood in the doorway. He looked at me for a moment, said nothing and walked away.

Barbara marched to the front door, slammed it shut as hard as she could and said, 'Good riddance.' In a condescending tone, she said, 'Don't worry, you will see Daddy in a couple of days, once he is settled in the cess pit he will call home. Now go away while I use the phone.'

I went back upstairs to lose myself. Yay for being home. Nobody explained to me what the divorce was, why it happened or what happened. But then, what did I expect? Nobody ever explained anything to me.

I just knew that Dad moved out and Barbara was really happy about it. She called everyone she knew to tell them the news.

CHAPTER TWENTY-TWO
The Attack

Age 15

A couple of days later, I was put in a car to go and see Dad at his new place.

That day, he violently raped me. This was the first time he had done anything like that. The next morning, he did things and made me do things.

I'm not emotionally able to write about what happened on those days, so this chapter ends here.

CHAPTER TWENTY-THREE
The Aftermath

Age 15

The pain in my lower half was excruciating. It hurt to walk and the rest of my body was stinging and sore. I daren't show it though, because of the fear that he would attack me again. I just kept my head down and did as I was told, and hoped this hell would end soon.

Later that day, at the SavaCentre, I wimpishly asked if I could call Barbara. Dad asked why and I said, 'To tell her I'll be home today.'

'Fine,' he said, and put some coins in my hands. 'I'd better go and get you something to eat or she will be nagging me later that I never fed you.'

As he walked away, sheer panic ran through my veins. I needed Emma; I needed her to help me. I shakily picked up the phone, put the coins in and opened my book with the phone number written in the front cover. I had seen this phone number many times but this time, it was hard to read. My heart was beating so hard, it made the numbers jump and it was hard to focus. I dialled and Emma answered. I said I didn't have much time. I explained briefly what had happened and how scared I was and that I needed to get away. Emma said that I should find someone and tell them what had happened, but with tears in my eyes and shaking, I said, 'I can't, I'm too scared.'

Emma got cross and said, 'Don't be scared, do it, it's not right what's happened.'

I whispered again, 'I'm really scared.'

She said I would be OK and to just find someone, anyone. I asked her not to tell anyone because otherwise, he would hurt me more. She agreed and said, 'Go and find someone now and call me when you've done it.'

I quietly said, 'OK.' But as I looked around at the people rushing to and fro, I knew I couldn't just go up to anyone.

Before I had time to put the phone down, Dad grabbed my arm and said, 'Come on, what's taking so long?'

The fright from him touching me and being so close caused my bowels to open. He had a plastic bag and he shoved it in my hands and said, 'Here's your food, tell Barbara I gave you a proper dinner, and eat it before you get home, so she doesn't see it.'

We walked to the bus stop and the bus came almost instantly. Dad paid the bus driver and pushed me on. I peed myself when he touched me. As he walked away, he shouted back, 'Tell Barbara I'll call her at some point.'

I sat on the bus; my knickers were saturated and full of faeces. I could smell myself and I was I pretty sure the rest of the bus could too, but I had lost the will to care. I had lost any form of self-respect; that had been ripped away from me. I didn't truly understand what had happened, only that parts of me really hurt that had never hurt before and I knew what he had done was wrong, it felt so very wrong. I think I was in shock or traumatised because I couldn't think straight. I had never been scared like this before. This was a different kind of scared, a disturbed scared that touched my soul.

The bus ride home was a blur; the driver had to break me from a trance to tell me to get off.

I had a long walk home. I threw up several times on the way and was constantly twitching, all of me hurt. I was weak and dizzy, terrified with the memories of what had happened. I constantly looked over my shoulder because I thought he was following me, and was going to attack me and do it all again. I was sore inside and out, but I just kept walking as fast as my body would let me. I had to; I had to get as far away from him as possible. I had to get home.

When I got home, I walked in the front door.

Barbara said, 'Oh here she is. Fun at Daddy's, was it?' I just stood there; I didn't know what to do. Barbara said, 'What's that smell, is it you? Go and have a bloody shower, for fuck's sake.'

I went up the stairs, crying. I didn't take my clothes off or change my knickers, I didn't want to go anywhere near what had happened down there. I shut my door and got into bed, pulled the covers over my head and broke down completely.

I lay there for days. I was broken like I had never been before. The beatings were different, they healed. This time, I felt like I was broken from the inside out and that it wasn't going to heal.

A darkness came over me. My body was no longer mine and my mind kept reminding me of that.

I replayed over and over the act that rotted me to my core, reliving one painful attack after another. It felt like my life was slowly fading away. I lay in the same place, petrified, violated, sore and alone, curled in a ball, shaking uncontrollably, unable to stop the tears even if I wanted to. I hoped I would die, because I thought death would hurt less than this.

***

The end of the week was up. I had laid there with one day blurring into the next. Barbara didn't know why I hadn't eaten or gone downstairs. She never asked, she was selfish like that, and I was too broken to tell.

She came to my room and said, 'It stinks in here, smells like shit. What have you been doing?' She opened the curtains and the window wide, pushed the covers off me and said, 'Your school taxi will be here in an hour, get up and get ready.'

She went out and I crawled my way out of bed, my body aching from lying in the same position so long. I went to the airing cupboard and pulled out some clothes. I gently peeled my clothes off, leaving my knickers till last. In the bathroom, I finally took my knickers off, trying to avoid looking at my vagina. It still hurt, and if there was a lot of damage, I didn't want to see. I rolled the knickers up in my clothes and hid them at the very bottom of the washing basket. Being naked made me feel exposed and vulnerable, and I started to cry and felt panicky. I didn't like not having my knickers on. I could barely breathe, I felt like it was going to happen again. As I put the clean clothes on, I was shaking uncontrollably, I couldn't stop.

When I was dressed, I just lay on the floor and cried, and held the front of my body. He had hurt me in a new way, and destroyed me at the same time.

The taxi ride to school was uncomfortable. I didn't know who I was. I was this shell of a person now, it felt like I had been stripped down to nothing. My mind was a blank; it was like I had forgotten how to function. Emma was in the taxi; she was sent to collect me in case I had problems dealing with the divorce, so I would have someone to talk to. She tried to talk to me, asked me what happened, asked if I told someone because she didn't hear back from me. I didn't say anything. I had no words, just fragments of myself floating around. I just stared out the window of the car, watching everything blur past.

When we were back at school, I took my stuff to the dormitory. Emma put her arm around me and said, 'Are you going to be OK?' My insides shuddered as she touched me. I wiped away my tears and put my head down.

I put my things away then one of the staff pulled me to one side and said I needed to have a shower. I put my head down and shook it.

She said, 'Why don't you have a shower? You need one, you smell really ripe.' I didn't lift my head.

She got my arm in a grip and took me down the stairs, telling another member of staff that I refused to shower. I hated her touching me, I tried to wriggle free from the grip on my arm but it just got tighter. My brain couldn't handle the fact of being touched anymore; fireworks were going off in my head.

I lifted my head and shouted, 'Get off my arm.'

The staff member said, 'If you have a shower, I may consider letting go of your arm.'

Then, a thundercloud of anger erupted. I don't remember much about it, I was even too weak to fight, but the anger was still there. I attacked. I ended up face down on the floor with my arms and legs up my back and staff sitting on me, restraining me while I lay there sobbing. Emma came out of the dormitory and stood at the top of the stairs. She said she wanted to speak to the head teacher.

The next thing I know, I was in the office with the head teacher. She came and sat close to me, and took my hands in hers. I immediately pulled mine away.

'OK, OK,' she said softly. 'Do you want some water?'

I nodded, she got me a glass of water and sat back down next to me. She said Emma had told her something that I had said happened, and that they were serious allegations and that she wanted to check with me what had happened. She moved her chair so that she was in front of me. Leaning in close, she said softly that if something has happened, this was a safe place to talk about it. If something happened to me, something not normal, then I should tell her.

I stared at the carpet, all brown and gold fuzzy squiggles going in all different directions, then I had flashbacks, one after the other, Dad's face saying, 'Don't tell or you will get hurt', all the times he bashed my face in, flashes of the blows I felt, the aggressive way he attacked me and raped me, going around in my mind like a slide show. My head was all confused, I felt sick. If I told her, it wouldn't make it stop, he would just kill me. The only difference was right now, in this moment, I didn't care if I lived or died. I was at the lowest I had ever been and I thought the end of my life was the only way to make it stop.

I hadn't said anything for a while and it's like she had read my thoughts. She put her hand under my chin and lifted my head slowly. She said, 'Do you want this to stop? Do you want the hurt to go away?' Tears rolled down my face as she spoke. 'There's only one way to make it stop,' she said, 'and that is to tell me. I can't help you if you don't tell me.'

Suddenly, it was like my brain broke and kept flashing up the rape over and over in my head, and I could feel the pain repeatedly in my body, the flashbacks wouldn't stop, his voice echoing round my head, making my head spin. I couldn't take any more.

Abruptly, I screamed, 'He hurt me. He hurt me a lot with his private parts. I tried to scream for help, I did, but I couldn't, he forced his hand over my mouth.'

I put my hands over my face and broke down into them. She put her arms round me and hugged me while I cried, saying, 'Oh no, you poor thing. It's OK, no one's going to hurt you now, you're OK.'

When I eventually calmed down, she got a tissue and wiped my face, then took my hand and explained it was OK for her to touch me because she wasn't going to hurt me. She put her hand out for me to hold, and when my hand was finally in hers, she gave it a gentle squeeze. She walked me to the office across the hall and asked the secretary to call the police please and send them to her office when they arrived.

When we were back in her office, she sat me down again and said, 'I'm not going to hurt you, OK, but what has happened is very bad and it can't happen again, so the police are going to come and talk to us to make sure that it doesn't happen again. I will sit here with you, and you need to tell them exactly what happened to you. Can you do that?' I shrugged my shoulders weakly. She said,' I will hold your hand while you talk. Will that make it feel easier to talk?'

'Yes,' I said.

'OK,' she said, 'I will do that.'

I didn't want to though; I just wanted it to go away. I had never spoken to a police person before, and it was hard enough telling the head teacher what had happened.

The policewoman turned up and sat in the room with me and the head teacher. I sat there while she asked me about my home life. I answered the questions as best I could, but didn't answer if she asked about me being hurt. I was still scared because I had already told and Dad had clearly told me not to.

She said I needed to tell her about some of the rape because she had to write it down. The hardest part was telling her about the actual rape because trying to explain it while you're reliving it in your head and crying hysterically is a hard thing to do.

The head teacher had tears in her eyes while I tried to explain. She wiped them away with a tissue. She then came over and gently hugged me, rocking at the same time. She explained that this should never have happened to me, that it was an evil thing he had done and that it wasn't my fault and did I understand that. I shook my head. I didn't really understand a lot of what was going on at that moment. I didn't know who I was anymore. All I knew was that I didn't want to be this broken and I didn't want it to happen again.

The police left and the head teacher headed me out to the showers and said that I needed to wash. I told her that I was scared to be naked and I didn't want to look at myself down there because of the pain. She said that was OK, and that how about if she stood in there and talked to me, not in the actual shower but in the same room around the corner, and she would speak to me to show me I wasn't alone, and that I could wash my back and my arms and my face and my hair, and not worry about looking down there, that I could just wash the rest of me. The way she made it sound, didn't seem that scary.

So, we went into the showers and I got into the shower cubicle and gently climbed out of my clothes. True to her word, she started talking, just random things, the things she liked. I remember her saying she liked smelling the fresh rain first thing in the morning, she loved the way summer made everyone happy. She liked picking shells off the beach and imagining all the creatures that had passed through that shell; she would imagine the stories that shell could tell. She liked the smell of cinnamon because it reminded her of Christmas, and how she liked to watch snow fall from her window while she held a steamy cup of hot chocolate.

I had never been to the beach, but I liked the smell of cinnamon too. It came to removing my knickers and I took a deep breath and carefully took them off and put them outside the cubicle on top of my clothes.

I stood under the shower and instantly, my body contorted from the shock of the water as it hit. It felt nice though; it felt like my muscles had wanted the relief of the water and appreciated it. I washed my arms and my face. I scrubbed hard to get every ounce of him off my skin. It felt like I could still feel him creeping on the surface. I bent down to scrub my legs and I looked. I didn't mean to look, I hated it, my vagina was broken and I was scared of how broken.

I felt dirty and I couldn't scrub him away. It felt like I still had the smell of him on me; I could smell it, I could feel it. I kept scrubbing and scrubbing. I stood in the shower, unable to define what was tears and what was water. Sobbing, I freaked out and cowered in the corner of the shower with my knees up, my head on my arms as the water cascaded over me, terrified.

The head teacher called out, but I couldn't get up. I just wanted to stop living this nightmare.

She came in, turned the shower off, helped me up and wrapped a towel around me. I broke down again, crying, and she said, 'I know, I know. We are going to fix this.'

I was taken to a single bedroom in the school, away from the dormitory. She said it would be better for me this way. She gave me some tomato soup and bread, which I devoured. It burnt my throat and tongue but I didn't even care, I was so hungry. It had been days since I had last eaten. The sheets in the bed were so clean and snug, that's all I cared about. I got into bed and that's where I stayed.

A couple of days later, I had to go for an internal examination at the doctors. The head teacher took me there and again, said that I would be safe with her. I sort of trusted her, but was still unsure. The doctor said she could wait with me but she couldn't come in for the examination. We waited and then I was asked to come in.

I was so scared in the room; my heart beat so fast and my palms were sweaty. I didn't know what was going to happen. A male doctor came over and asked that I take off my bottoms and my knickers and put on these paper knickers, and then pointed where I could change.

I had to lie on a table with the paper knickers on. The doctor said he would put things in my vagina and at the same time, check to see if there was damage. He asked if I was OK with that. I didn't answer; my whole body was shaking violently and there was nothing I could do to calm it.

The doctor said, 'I know you're scared. OK, I'll be as gentle as I can.'

All I know is that every time the doctor put an instrument inside me, it felt like I was being raped all over again. I tried to shut my legs, push myself up off the table to get away from the pain. Then I cried while I lay there until it was finished.

The drive back to school was a quiet one. I was petrified again. I just wanted to be alone. The head teacher kept saying that I had done the right thing and that everything was going to be OK now.

I didn't feel OK; I was scared, scared of doctors, scared of people. So much had happened since I had said what had happened, and it was so much to try and process.

***

A few weeks went past and I was allowed to stay in the single room by myself all day if I wanted to. They thought it was best that I didn't mingle with the other children because of the state I was in.

Emma would pop in and see me and tell me things that were going on at school and ask me when I was going to come back and join them. I didn't really know what was going to happen so I didn't answer her.

The head teacher had told me that because of the results of the internal examination, my dad had now been arrested. I was even more scared now; he would definitely know that I had told. He would be so mad.

A week later, it was time to go home for a few weeks. In the taxi, Emma said her goodbyes and hugged me, promising she would call. I got out of the taxi and headed to the front door. I went in and Barbara was standing in the living room.

'A lot's been going on while you've been at school,' she said in a strangely joyful tone. 'I'll tell you, like I told the police people that came to the house, I knew it. I knew he was going to rape you. I always knew it was just a matter of time.' She said that so proudly, like she was an all-knowing saviour for having this great information. She said, 'Are you going to tell me what happened then?'

'No,' I said, and headed upstairs.

I heard her shout behind me, 'Well that's lovely, isn't it?'

Barbara had the neighbours over a few times and I could hear her from my bedroom, telling them the information that she knew, and explaining how she was the victim, that she had lived with a monster all that time and that, at any moment, he could have done it to her, and how lucky everyone who lived on the street was that he hadn't done it to their little girl.

I didn't think my life was going to get any worse, but a week later, it did.

There was a phone call from the school, saying that it was government funded and that the funding had now been stopped and the school was to close down, and so we could no longer to return.

I felt a massive hole in the pit of my stomach and my brain span a little bit. I liked the school, it was like my sanctuary. What about Emma? Would I ever see her again?

I was beside myself; it was news that tore me apart. Barbara didn't look too happy either.

I asked to phone Emma. Barbara agreed and I phoned Emma, and we both cried and said that somehow, we would get to see each other again. We said we would still write when we could. It was sad news for both of us, and by the end of the phone call, we must have said goodbye 50 times or more because neither of us wanted to hang up.

I went back to my room and just sat in shock, completely unaware of where my life was about to take me.

Witness Statement

(CJ Act 1967 s.9; MC Act 1980 ss.5A, (3) (a) and 5B. MC Rules 1981 r.70)

Statement of   Mrs

Age if under 18   'O'18   (if over 18 insert "over 18")   **Occupation**

This statement (consisting of 13 pages each signed by me) is true to the best of my knowledge and belief and I make it knowing that, if it is tendered in evidence, I shall be liable to prosecution if I have wilfully stated in it anything which I know to be false or do not believe to be true.

Signature   Date 20.7.98

On March the 6th 1985 I moved into the staff quarters after leaving my husband and as I've stated began a friendship with Mr

This friendship then led into a relationship which in the beginning I would describe as a normal happy one.

In October 1986 Mr. attended Family Court to be granted sole care of child as her mother had not applied for access.

Then in November 1986 Mr and I married at St Albans registry office and at that time we were still living in the flat.

However in June 1987 we moved into a cottage again in the grounds of the hospital and it was at that point to my mind that our marriage began to deteriorate. Mr started to become violent towards me causing numerous bruises to my body and breaking my nose on two separate occasions.

Until then Mr's drinking had been substantial but controlled however it became steadily worse.

I should state that I have suffered bouts of depression throughout my life which returned during the incidents of domestic violence.

In 1992 Mr and child and I moved to our current address. It was around this time that Mr drinking became steadily worse and whilst the domestic violence stopped the verbal abuse and threats worsened.

Over the years of our marriage I left Mr numerous times often staying in a women's refuge and friends' houses, however I would always return, my concern being for child who would have been left with Mr

Mr rarely in my view had time for child particularly when he'd been drinking. When I was there he would often tell me to shut her up and get her out of his way. Often child heard him but always remained loyal to him.

Mr and I separated, he left the home and was allocated a room in a hostel pending being rehoused by the council.

I had by that time sought advice from a solicitor who had served Mr with papers regarding a judicial separation, a residence order for child and sole tenancy of the house.

Following this particular incident I spoke to Mr and we agreed that child could spend a weekend with him to give me a break. We agreed that she would sleep in Mr. friends room next door to his as he was going away for the weekend.

Child eventually arrived home in a taxi around 7 p.m. that evening she looked very tired and told me that she hadn't had a lot of sleep as she'd had sickness and diarrhoea.

At that time given child still seemed tired and was still complaining of a stomach ache I was not unduly concerned.

Child went back to school as normal

Then at 7.50p.m. on Tuesday (9.6.98) I telephoned the school to be told by a member of staff that the headteacher wanted to speak to me before I spoke to child and that she would call me as soon as possible.

During the conversation she told me that child had told the Head of Care, and herself that her father had raped her.

Initially I couldn't take in what they'd told me but my immediate response was that she was medically examined to make sure she wasn't damaged in any way. We also agreed that child should stay at school for the stability and security.

THE AFTERMATH

CONSTABULARY

Record of Tape Recorded Interview
with
Mr.
on
WEDNESDAY 8TH JULY 1998

Interviewing Officers:

Other persons present: None

Place of Interview: Police Station

Time Interview Commenced: 15:06 hours

Time Interview Concluded: 16:34 hours

Tape Reference No:

Q. Why you don't want a solicitor?

A. I don't really know what I'm... whether I'm actually getting charged with anything or not, so I mean...

Q. Yeah? And can you tell us why you feel okay, for us to speak to you without a solicitor?

A. Well, I don't think I've done anything wrong.

Q. Yeah? What was the reason for your separation?

A. Just me and Mrs weren't getting on and we decided one had to go so I decided I'd... I'd be the one to

Q. Okay. So while you were with Mrs and while child was growing up what was your relationship like with child ?

A. Okay. I've never had any trouble. That's why I can't understand this.

Q. Right, okay. So would you say you got to spend a lot of time with child?

A. No, no more than anybody else.

Q. And your relationship with her was good?

A. Yes.

Q. Bad, indifferent?

A. No. I've always got on with her. I can't... that's what I say.

Q Yes.

A. No. I've always got on with her. I've always got on with her

Q. Hm.

A. She's... We used to walk around the town and she'd say, "Oh, I've got two mummies", so she's always known that Mrs is not her proper mother.

Q. Hm. And what...? As I said, how did the separation of you and Mrs affect child would you say?

A. I don't suppose she likes it for one minute but, as I said, we explained to her what was happening and there was... there wasn't really a lot we could do about it.

Q. Right. When you and Mrs discussed child staying over...

A. Yeah.

Q. ... where was it that she was going to be sleeping?

THE AFTERMATH

A. Well, I... I told Mrs   that she could sleep in the bed and I'd sleep in the chair, that's what...

Q. Right. Okay. So you say it was on a Saturday when you weren't working a couple of months ago. Can you be any more specific than that at all?

A. Well, I'm saying not... not really with dates.

Q. Right. So... and what happened from there?

A. We just went to into the room, watched a bit of tele, went out, had something to eat, then come back and watched some more tele, as far as I remember. That was it.

Q. And what happened from there?

A. I can't... You know, it's... not being funny but not having had time to think about it really.

Q. So what... what time would you have gone to sleep?

A. Don't really know. It's very hard to say really.

Q. Right. So I'm not wishing to be, like, tricky or... or funny about this at all but what you're saying is that you've sat, you had... been out for your lunch, you've gone back to your room and you've sat for something like six to eight hours just watching television and then you've gone to sleep.

A. Well, child bought some videos anyway, or her own videos.

Q. She bought her own videos?

A. Bought some videos, if I remember rightly.

Q. Right.

A. And watched the videos.

Q. Can you remember what videos she brought?

A. No.

Q. Right. Just quickly. When you did go over to the... The pub I know this will be really stretching your memory but can you remember what you had for lunch at all?

A. No.

Q. No? Can you remember whether you had a drink while you were there?

A. Oh yeah. I... I had a beer anyway, yeah.

Q. Right. Okay. So that afternoon you've had a couple of pints down at the pub. Then you have a few cans in the house, or in your room. How many cans that Saturday are we talking about, roughly?

A. What, did I drink?

Q. Hm.

A. Haven't got a clue.

Q. Right. Okay. Two, four, 10, 15?

A. It's hardly to say really. I mean...

Q. Was you drinking out of the ordinary that

A. No.

Q. ...particular Saturday?

A. No.

Q. So how many usually on a Saturday would you drink?

A. I don't know. I can't put a figure on it.

Q. Right, okay.

A. I don't sort of count 'em as I'm drinking 'em.

Q. Okay. So you watched the TV, watched the videos, had a few drinks, child was watching her videos. Were you watching them with her?

A. Well, that and reading papers and...

Q. Right.

A. Wasn't sort of taking that much notice, I don't think.

Q. And then you said you went to bed between 10.00 and 12.00. When you got to your chair that night can you remember feeling whether you'd had a few too many to drink or were you okay?

A. I was okay.

Q. You were all right?

A. Yeah.

Q. Right. So you slept all night in the chair. How did you sleep? Did you sleep well, that's what I'm saying to you?

A. Oh yeah, yeah.

Q. You slept well in the chair? Then you woke up about what time?

A. I don't know. The following morning. I don't know. Haven't got a clue.

Q. Okay. What happened the next morning? What happened?

A. Took her back, as far as I know. We just caught the bus and went back, back to Mrs

Q. She says at this point that she was scared and she was telling you to go away and that she said that she's seen you get angry with

149

Mum before and, as I say, she was scared and she was, just telling you you should go away. She says, she describes you as an alcoholic. She says "He always drinks can after can and he drinks big cans" and that the day that she'd come round to see you there was a fridge full of beer and that there was no food. What do you say? Would that be a...?

A. Well, I mean, I always keep beers in me fridge anyway 'cos, I mean, I don't hardly ever go out anyway, so... (Inaudible) I mean, I've... I've had a few dreers... beers. I mean, I must admit, I mean, I don't... there's nowhere I go. You know, it's just me, the room and basically television.

Q. Okay. She's saying that you already had your clothes off when you got into bed in the afternoon, yeah, and that your pants were taken off at some stage under the duvet. After she says that you tried to put your penis inside her she said that she was trying to get up but she couldn't. She said that she knew that your penis had gone inside her because she felt it and that it hurt and that afterwards she was sore.

A. No. I'm not being funny but (Inaudible) any of this.

Q. Okay. She describes your penis at the time being straight and hard, and she's saying that she hasn't seen your penis before, she'd never seen it before, this was the first time that she'd seen it. She's actually said that nothing like this has ever happened before, that this has been the first occasion that something like this has happened.

A. I can only by what she's... go by what she's said. : mean, I don't know.

Q. Right. When... when all of this was going on she also said that you tried to kiss her on the mouth but she told you to go away No?

A. No.

Q. No attempts to kiss her on the mouth at all?

A. Not as far as I know anyway.

Q. Hm. She said that before she'd left you had said to Not to tell anybody about what had happened and that she'd gone home, and she said she was too scared to tell her mum in case her mum got upset and angry, and the first person she told was a schoolfriend and that then she'd told a member of staff at her school a couple of weeks later. Then she said that you've never done anything like this before.

A. That's what I can't understand why this has come about.

Q. I am very convinced that what she's telling us is the truth. She is telling us some very, very serious allegations and I am convinced she is telling us the truth.

A. As I say, I don't know.

Q. Which is serious, very serious. And you can't give any explanation

A. No.

Q. So she's got nothing to gain. It's like already said. All she's going to do is just lose out of this situation, isn't she? She wasn't, she didn't run to the police to give this evidence or to tell us about it. She told a friend who told a teacher and she's very, very disturbed and upset about the whole thing, and rightly so.

A. What does Mrs say?

Q. Mrs is quite behind her, very behind her. You... we don't get 15 year old girls coming to us and lying like this...

A. Well, I don't know.

Q. ... in such detail as this, to go into, she's gone to, into minute detail about things that have happened, what she was wearing, how you tried to undo her bra, how you tried to have sex with her.

A. As I say, as far as I'm concerned, I don't... I... You know, I haven't done it.

Q. So what she's saying is a total bunch of lies then?

A. Well, that's what, that's what I said. I don't know why.

Q. But that's what you're saying. Everything that's happened or what

A. Yeah, it must be, yeah.

Q. Right. child 's described to us the sleeping arrangements as she said happened on that Saturday evening and the clothes you were wearing and she was wearing, okay? I now need for you to go through exactly where you slept, what you slept in, where child slept and the same, what clothes she slept in. Can you go through...?

A. Well, as far as I'm concerned, she slept on the... I slept on the chair and she slept in the bed.

Q. Right. And what did you wear? What were you wearing?

A. I was just wearing me clothes.

Q. Right. So when child got to bed, went to bed that evening, what happened, the, the ritual, the bedtime ritual?

A. Well, as far as I was con... concerned, she just said she was... "I'm going to bed" and I was just sitting there watching the television and she just got into bed. I didn't take any notice of her.

Q. Did she get undressed? Did she bring her pyjamas with her, clean her teeth, go to the toilet?

A. I'm not sure. (Pause) I can't actually remember. I didn't take much notice of her getting into bed, no.

Q. No. At any time during that night did you actually get into the bed, on the bed with child?

A. No.

Q. Either consciously or unconsciously and then wake up knowing you're there?

A. No.

Q. None at all?

A. No.

Q. Okay. You woke up the next morning and were still in the chair?

A. Yeah.

Q. This is the first time child has ever stayed at your bedsit.

A. Yeah.

Q   And you're now saying you can't remember it or you can't remember it in detail?

A. No. I mean, to start with.

A. I can remember bits and pieces.

Q. Hm.

A. Nothing. I can't remember what I done last weekend, so I mean, it's not... nothing new, is it?

Q. Why can't you remember?

A. No, 'cos I just don't, don't think of it. I just do it and...

Q. How much had you drunk that weekend?

A. Don't know. As I said, I was drinking in general.

Q. But did you know everything you were doing that weekend?

A. Well, not now, 'cos, I mean, I can't remember what I was doing that weekend. I mean, I know I went out for lunch.

Q. You can give us no explanation?

A. No.

Q. Nothing at all?

A. No. As far as I'm concerned it, it didn't happen.

Q. There is just one other point, the teacher who child first spoke to... remembers an incident, I believe it was last year, where she'd come into school and she was just talking about things in general and she told this teacher that she'd woke up one night at home in bed and that you were sitting in the room watching her, and she said nothing more about this other than she thought it was odd, child thinking it was odd.

A. Well, Mrs must have been there.

Q. Has there ever been a time when you've sat in child's room just watching her while she was asleep?

A. No

Q. So there was never, ever in the whole time you've been together an opportunity for you to do that

A. Well, (inaudible} I don't know why I'd do it if I did do..

4. On 3 July 1998 another Memorandum interview was held facilitated by of Social Services at which child made full disclosures. Mr was subsequently arrested and charged.

5. On 8 July 1998 child underwent a full medical examination by a Police Surgeon in

Other Causes for Concern

1. As mentioned above, child has been a pupil at Greenwood School since she was 11. She feels secure at this school, has friends and clearly feels well supported by various staff members. I visited the school with Mrs on 22 July 1998, the day before the end of term in order to meet the Head Teacher and all seemed well.

   However, on 29 July 19981 received information from Mrs that the school had been closed with immediate effect.

REASONS FOR CPC

Child told a member of staff at school that she had been raped by her father whilst staying with him during the weekend of 30th/31st May. She has been medically examined and interviewed, and Mr has been arrested and charged. This CPC was convened to consider whether child remains at risk of abuse, and if so, whether a Protection Plan is necessary to ensure her protection. It was noted that only

THE AFTERMATH

Mr has parental responsibility for child and Mrs is planning to make an application for a Residence Order.

PART 3

LIFE AFTER SCHOOL

9 months later

CHAPTER TWENTY-FOUR
Court Case

Age 15

Barbara told me that we were going to court that day and that I had to tell some more people what happened. The police explained what was happening to her instead of me, as she had told them I was mental. I didn't really know what court was, I didn't understand the whole procedure or what it meant. I just knew that because of court, I hadn't been allowed to talk to Emma because she was a witness, as I had told her what happened that day. Someone told me I could talk to her again once the court case was over. It had been months since I had spoken to her, even longer since I had seen her.

I told Barbara that I didn't want to go to court, that I was scared and I just wanted to be alone. I didn't care about anything. If the whole world collapsed around me, I would still be happy to just lie in my bed alone.

Barbara pulled me up by my shoulders, slapped my face hard and said, 'You have to do this. This is the last time you will have to tell anybody, today. It's very important that you speak. Now get up and get dressed,

I'll wait for you downstairs. I'll be calling a taxi in 20 minutes.'

I sat on the edge of my bed and cried. I didn't understand why I couldn't just lie there. My clothes were scattered on the floor. I picked up the nearest things and put them on, and sat there for a minute or two, just staring into space. It felt so hard to even think properly, so many things had happened. Trying to process it all was way too much. I stood up and walked downstairs.

The taxi pulled up outside the crown court. It was a large building with a big coat of arms emblem mounted on the front. I stared up at it as it towered above me. Barbara paid the taxi driver and we headed in. There were security people everywhere. We were stopped in the foyer and Barbara explained who we were and why we were there. We got taken to a room that reminded me of a doctor's waiting room, with square, padded, metal chairs in a circle against the wall and two tables in the middle, piled with magazines.

We were told to wait in there until we were called. I sat on the chair at the top end of the room; Barbara chose the chair at the far end of the room, so we were sitting at opposite ends of the room to each other.

Barbara got up and picked up a few magazines, put them on the chair beside her and started to read one. I looked round the room. On the right was the door we had just come in and on the same wall was a huge, rectangular window. I don't know if that was for us to look out or for other people to look in, but I couldn't see anything out there from where I was sitting. A white clock ticked on another wall. It was 9:50a.m. I couldn't remember the last time I knew the time or what day it was, but I didn't suppose that mattered.

I watched it in the silence; the ticking sound seemed louder and louder as it echoed through the room. There was something truly mesmerising about watching the second-hand tick round, the sound of it in turn with the movement sucked me in. The noise of the ticking was very annoying but also hypnotic.

A lady came in and said my name. I looked at her and then at the clock; it said 11:10a.m. Had I been looking at that clock all that time? I looked back at her.

She said, 'Sorry to keep you, if you would like to come with me.'

Barbara stood, so I stood. I waited for Barbara to start walking so I could follow, but she didn't. I looked over at her, but she was not moving.

She said, 'It's just you, go on,' but I stayed standing. I was scared, I didn't know where I was going. I sat back down and cried my eyes out. The lady who was at the door sat down next to me. She put her hand on my arm and I flinched so she immediately took it away.

She said softly, 'It's OK, don't be scared. You are going to come with me and I'm going to take you to a room with two people in it. There, you are going to tell them what happened and then I will come and get you and bring you back here. Then you can go home. Easy-peasy. Do you think you can do that for me? You won't be left alone, I promise. Little steps, one at a time. So, shall we try step one, can you take my hand?'

I had stopped crying at this point and was just listening to her. I didn't want to take her hand so I said, 'No.'

'Can you walk with me to the door?' I nodded, she stood up and then I stood up. She reached into her pocket and brought out a tissue, held it out and said, 'For your eyes.' I took it and held it in my hand tightly.

We walked through corridors until we came to a door. She knocked and a happy voice said, 'Come in.'

Inside, there was a man sitting on a table with some recording equipment and a blonde lady sitting on a swivel chair with a mini TV on the table in front of her. She greeted me and asked me to sit on the chair next to her, which was directly facing the mini TV. My chair didn't swivel, it was like the ones in the waiting room. The TV was off, the screen was blank. The woman who had brought me to the room said she would be back later and wished me goodbye as she shut the door.

The woman on the swivel chair said her name was Claire and asked if I knew what was going on. I shook my head.

She brought her swivel chair as close to me as she could and said in a kind voice, 'OK, let me explain. This is court and you will have to explain what happened to you. A man will appear on the screen,' she pointed to the TV, 'then once you have explained your story, there will be a 15 to 20-minute break when you can sit and relax and drink some water. Then, another man will come on the screen and ask you more questions about what happened. He may seem a bit mean and unfair, but it's his job to ask all the questions. You have to talk into the

TV because you are only 15. If you are older, you would normally be in the actual court room. Also, when you leave here, you are not allowed to say to anyone anything you will have said in this room today or what was asked. You can't talk to anyone who is involved in the court case until it's over, just in case they influence you or vice versa. I know this is going to be really hard, but you're doing the right thing. I know this is a lot of information to take in, but I'm here if you have any questions at all. Do you have any questions?'

'Is my dad here?'

The woman leaned into me and said, 'I don't know if he is here.'

'If I speak again, he will get me after. He told me not to say anything, he will get me. He said he will get me!' I put my hands over my face and cried.

Claire put her hand on my shoulders. She said, 'Hey, hey, he is not going to get you, I will make sure of it. You're doing this to make sure he doesn't get you. This is a massive thing you are doing, and you are so brave for doing it.' She asked the man who had been sitting silently the whole time to hand her some tissues. 'Hey, lift your head.' I lift my head and she wipes the tears from my eyes. 'I know you're scared, but all you have to do is say what you know, I'll be here with you the whole time, I'm not going anywhere. Take a few deep breaths, get nice and calm, I'll get you a big glass of water and you let me know when you're ready to begin.'

She came back with the water. I took big gulps, I was so thirsty; I was hungry too and really tired. The crying had made me tired, I just wanted to go home, I just wanted it to end, hadn't I been through enough already?

After a few minutes, Claire asked if I was ready. In my head, I knew I was never going to be ready, but I nodded anyway.

She turned on the TV and there was a snowy screen, a mass of black and white pixels, fighting among themselves to make a picture. Claire pushed another button and then a man was on the screen. He had a white, trimmed beard and was maybe early 50s. The clothes I could see he was wearing were black, and he had a white, plaited headpiece on. He was very serious but pleasant. He explained that he was a judge and that I would have to tell him what happened to me. He said that he wanted me to be as comfortable as possible and that some people found his wig too intimidating and that he was happy to take it off if I wanted him to.

I looked at Claire. She mouthed, 'It's OK.' I shook my head at the judge, so he left the wig on.

He said, 'If you need a break, you tell Claire and we will stop. Is that OK? Do you understand?' I nodded. He continued, 'In your own time, tell me exactly what happened that night, start from the beginning, before you got there.'

I swallowed hard, drank some more water and started panicking inside, my heart was pounding. I looked at Claire and she smiled at me. I started to explain everything that had happened, starting from the beginning, like he had asked. I could feel myself shaking inside as I was telling it. The judge nodded and occasionally spoke when he wanted something explained in more depth or to know how something had happened. My tears kept falling while I spoke, but I just kept brushing them away, determined to tell him what happened on those awful days, telling myself in my head that I just had to tell him what happened and that's it, then I could go home.

My throat was so dry towards the end and picking up the glass of water was so hard because I was shaking so much. My heart was beating so fast and hard that it was making all of the other parts of my body beat along with it. Then it was done. I finished saying what had happened, the judge thanked me for the information I had given and told me that we could all now have a 20-minute break. The screen went blank.

'Well done. I knew you could do it,' Claire said, and went to get me some more water. I felt relief, like a massive weight had been lifted.

I went to the toilet and as I sat, my legs shook uncontrollably. I tried to calm myself but it was so hard. I put my face in my hands and cried and cried. I had just relived what had happened again and it was awful remembering it stage by stage. Remembering the pain, the helplessness, the aggression all of it.

A little knock on the door came. It was Claire. 'Are you OK in there? We are about to start.' I finished and opened the door.

As we walked back to the room, Claire said, 'Only this last bit and you are all finished. This bit is going to seem really hard, but it will be OK. Remember, you did the last bit, so you can do this bit, I know you can do it.'

I sat down in the chair. Claire said, 'Ready?' and I nodded. The TV flickered on and there was a different

167

man on the screen. This time, he was youngish, around mid-30s, clean-shaven, but also wearing a headpiece. He didn't seem as pleasant.

He stated his name, but I didn't catch it because he was talking quite fast. He said throughout, he was going to ask me questions about that day and the day after. He then started to talk about what I'd said. He tried to turn what I had said around and portray it from a different angle, then he asked me questions that I had to answer. Immediately after I answered each question, he would imply I was a liar. He would then ask another question, and then turn the answer I gave upside down and make it something else.

He was constantly changing what I had said, and telling me what he thought had happened. I was confused because he spoke so fast and sometimes, he did not even give me enough time to finish my sentence properly.

I told him, 'But it didn't happen like that.' I said how it really happened.

He would go on to say quickly, 'How do we know it happened like that? Maybe it happened like this. Are you sure it happened like that?'

It went on.

'Are you sure, with your dad's history of violence, you didn't know that this could happen?

'Are you sure you had no indication this would happen when you left the house that afternoon?'

'Why didn't you run?'

'Why didn't you leave the room?'

'When you screamed, why did no one come?'

'Did you even scream like you say you did?'

'Why did you phone Emma and not Barbara?'

'Why didn't you tell someone, like Emma had told you to do?'

By this stage, I was really uncomfortable. I could feel tears splashing onto my cheeks. I didn't know the answers to the questions; I didn't know why. He kept confusing me and changing my words. He asked me more questions. I sat there saying nothing. I didn't know what to say. He looked at me and said, 'Your silence speaks volumes.'

'Maybe it didn't happen how you said it had.'

'Maybe it didn't happen at all.'

'Maybe you had made it all up.'

'Why did you wait so long to tell someone?'

'Why didn't you tell someone straight away?'

He kept saying more and more things. I couldn't understand why he had to say those things when I had already told the first man what happened, or why this man was so nasty. It all got too much for me. I was confused, upset and angry.

I stood up and screamed at the screen, 'I told you what happened. I told you the truth. I don't know anything else.'

I sat on the floor crying, my knees bent up with my head tucked into them, rocking backwards and forwards, while my hands violently gripped big clumps of my hair and I sobbed my heart out. I felt Claire stand up and tell me that we were going to have a break. While I sat there, hyperventilating and whining between sobs, she sat down beside me and rubbed my back, saying, 'It's OK, you did OK.'

In the Crown Court

at

Case No.
Court Code.

Certificate of Conviction or Finding
Sex Offenders Act 1997 s.5(2)

Name	Mr.
Address	
Date of Birth	
Date of conviction/finding	*17/2/99*
Convicting court if different	
Date of sentence if different	
Offence(s) and sentence(s)	*RAPE* *SENTENCE 7 YEARS* *IMPRISONMENT*

I hereby certify that the above named defendant was on the above date [convicted] [found not guilty by reason of insanity] [found to be under a disability and to have done the act charged against him] in respect of the above sexual offence(s) to which Part 1 of the Sex Offenders Act 1997 applies: and that the court so stated in open court on that date.

An Officer of the Crown Court
Date *17/2/99*

For immediate service: CPS/Police/Prison (etc)/Hospital/Local Authority/Probation/court file
Copy for the Defendant *(who should be asked to sign below)*

Defendants signature   Date *17/2/99*

CHAPTER TWENTY-FIVE
Alice

Age 16

It had been one year since the court case, where Dad was sentenced to seven years in prison. I was still living with Barbara.

Dad had never spoken of my real mother to me. I think he wanted me to believe that Barbara was my real mother, but I always knew she wasn't.

One afternoon, Barbara shouted up the stairs that someone was on the phone for me. With the whirlwind of the last year, I was nervous and a little bit apprehensive about who was calling. I took the phone and an unfamiliar voice told me he was the doctor of my birth mother, Alice, and that she was dying and had been for a little while, and this was maybe her last few months to live. He said she wanted to see me before she died.

The conversation was a bit of a blur. I caught bits every now and then, but all I could hear in my head was that my mum wanted me, she had come back after all this time and we were going to be together, we were going to be a family, finally.

At that moment, my heart swelled with love. After I put the phone down, I stood for I don't know how long, my head buzzing with all sorts of different things, different scenarios of how we would meet, what she would say, her reasons for not coming back sooner. How she would say she loved me and always loved me, and how sorry she was and that she should never have given me up and how she had regretted it every single day since. I imagined that she would pack up my things from Barbara's and I would take my rightful place and move in with her, and the horrible things that happened to me would be a distant memory because she would make everything right again. I would have my mum back for good.

I took myself upstairs and sat on my bed thinking, my brain in conflict with itself. First, I felt heart-swelling happiness, then reality hit and I remembered she was dying, and that she had abandoned me. The war waged like this:

She is dying, I should see her.

No, why should I see her? She only wants to see me now she is dying; she made no effort before that.

Why didn't she want to see me while she was well? Why couldn't she phone me herself? She had plenty of opportunities but she waited until now.

Where was she when I needed her the most?

She could have protected me, but she didn't.

She didn't even try, not even once.

All the questions went around and round in my head. I didn't know what I was supposed to do. I didn't know what I wanted to do. I knew what I thought I always wanted to do, but that was under different circumstances.

When I imagined the day I would actually meet her, I never thought she would be dying.

A part of me wanted to see her and have her tell me that she was sorry, that she always loved me and she tried to come and find me but she couldn't find me. The other part of me was saying: *you gave me up and a lot of bad things have happened because you weren't there to protect me, you don't deserve to see me.*

Barbara came into my room. I hadn't heard her come up the stairs with all the thoughts blasting through my head. She sat on my bed and asked me what I was going to do. I said I didn't know. She said to me, 'Your mum was never there. She dropped you as a baby and ran. She gave up her responsibility. She never wanted you; you just got in the way of her life. I have looked after you all these years, washed your clothes, fed you, and stayed with your dad. I didn't have to, you know, I could have left at any time. Where was she?' With that, she got up and went downstairs.

I felt bad because Barbara was trying to give me the guilt treatment. I thought about my life with her. Being the size she was, she could have stopped a lot of Dad's violent abuse. She never read me a story at bedtime, gave me a cuddle or any compassion. And yes, I blamed her for the rape. I blamed everyone: Dad for doing it, Barbara for sending me there, and my birth mother for not being here. I blamed myself for not being strong enough to fight him off.

I sat on the edge of the bed and thought for a while longer.

I decided I would see my birth mum. It couldn't be anything worse than what I had been through already, and I was desperate to be loved. She had to love me, she was my mother.

A week later, I got on a bus and headed to the nursing home. I tried to conjure up the compassion that was needed for the day of the meeting, but how could I conjure up feelings that were not there, when I felt confused and angry with that woman my whole life.

I had a vision of her in my mind, a perfect person, very pretty with wealth and manners. My mother would be the sort of person that everyone loves. Leaving me must have been out of her control. She couldn't find me, even though she searched and searched. She always thought of me every day and needed me back.

How wrong I was.

The nursing home was a big building, a hospital with lots of rooms made into bedrooms.

A nurse asked my name and took me into one of the bedrooms. It had a bed, toilet and a chair in the corner. There was a woman sitting in the middle of the room in a wheelchair and a man sitting on the edge of the bed, talking to her. His face showed complete horror when he saw me. He leapt to his feet and rushed out of the room; his suddenness startled me. He obviously recognised me, but I had no idea who he was.

The nurse explained to Alice who I was.

I stared, unable to look away. The mother that left me that day was sitting in front of me in a wheelchair, wearing a nappy, delirious, and basically looking like death was sitting on her shoulder, just waiting to take her sorry self away. She was frail and skinny, and she was definitely not in a normal state of mind.

Alice started making sounds like she was trying to make words but none of them made any sense. The nurse explained that she had a brain and muscle-wasting disease and couldn't walk, talk, or do anything for herself. She also had dementia so didn't know what was going on. A lot of the time, she didn't know who she or anybody else was.

I stared at her more, hoping to have something, a connection, a bond, an answer, anything...

But nothing. I was just looking at a stranger in a vegetative state.

How could this happen to her? It was so awful. She was so skinny and so frail that she looked like she would break if you touched her. My mind was confused. It was hard to get my head around how this woman could be my mother. She was only 39 but looked so much older.

Alice was moving her hand really slowly, as if she was trying to touch me.

The nurse looked on and said, 'I think she wants to hold your hand. You can give her your hand if you want to.'

I was nervous and scared to put my hand out. I didn't want to, it was all too strange. But I couldn't be horrible; I had to put my feelings aside for a moment, so I put my hand on the edge of the wheelchair. She slowly put her hand on top of mine. Then she started to make loud noises like a sea lion. I watched her face and she stared at me as her face contorted, tears falling from her eyes, shouting and howling nonsense words. I started to cry, mainly because I hated this and it scared the hell out of me. This wasn't how it was supposed to be, we were supposed to talk and hug and questions were supposed to be answered. This wasn't the way I imagined it, this was not my mum.

It was all too much. I ripped my hand away and shot out the door. I ran down the hall, past the rooms, down another corridor, out of the double doors, and let the cold, fresh air hit my teary face. I dropped to my knees and screamed as loud as I could. I felt like I was in a nightmare. I shouldn't have come. What a fool I was for thinking that I was finally owed a decent parent. My whole life, I had felt that she would save me in the end, that she would be the one to rescue me, but she couldn't even save herself.

After I had calmed down, I sat on the stony path, trying to make sense of everything. The same nurse came out of the double doors and stood next to me. She explained that it was always tough seeing someone like that for the first time, and that I had dealt with it really well. She handed me a piece of paper with the name 'Tom' and a phone number scrawled on it. She said that the man who had been with Alice when I arrived asked her to give it to me. He was Alice's husband and they also had a daughter together, my half-sister, and that he really wanted to speak to me. I stared down at the piece of paper, thoughts tumbling around in my head like crazy.

From all the crying, I could feel a headache coming fast. The nurse asked if I would like to come back inside and see her again. I put my head down and said no. I carried on staring at the piece of paper and started replaying the madness that had just happened in my head.

She had a brain and muscle-wasting disease that was eating away at her.

She had no recollection of the past so any questions I would have liked her to answer were long gone. She would take those answers to her grave with her.

I should have felt sorry for her but I didn't, because I had found out that after leaving me, she had remarried and then went on to have another daughter.

So here I was, feeling the burn of resentment I'd had all my life for her, followed up by the fact that I had been replaced.

Heartbroken doesn't even start to cover what I was feeling. The gaping void would now never be filled; it would just swallow me up instead.

I kept staring at the piece of paper, asking myself: Do I call the number?

CHAPTER TWENTY-SIX
Tom

Age 16

A few days had passed and I was still undecided whether or not to call Tom. I thought about my half-sister, and that maybe she could be a good thing. I thought that maybe Tom could give me the answers that I so desperately wanted. But I also worried that they might not be the answers I wanted. I didn't want to imagine another perfect situation, only to have it end up like the last one.

I threw the different options around in my head for a while, then I decided to be brave. I had come this far, I couldn't turn back now. I dialled the number, it rang, and a man's voice chirpily said, 'Hello.' I immediately slammed the phone down. My heart raced so fast, I could feel it in my throat.

I decided I was not ready to do it, and stuffed the piece of paper in a drawer. Then, the phone started ringing. I stared at it, knowing I shouldn't answer, but there was something inside, daring me to pick it up. I picked it up shakily and said, 'Hello.'

Tom said my name and asked if it was me.

'Yes. It's me.'

'I'm overwhelmed that you called. I didn't think you would.'

He did a lot of talking so it didn't feel so awkward. He said he wanted to meet and explain a few things to me about Alice. He asked whether I would be OK to meet up. I thought to myself that as I was halfway there, I might as well carry on. We agreed to meet that very afternoon at a pub.

I panicked on the way to the pub.

Was he going to bring my half-sister to see me?

What was he going to say?

Had this all been a sick joke and he would say, 'Your mum is alive and well,' and bring her with him?

Would he explain how she got ill?

Was she ill when she gave me up?

Did I make her ill and was that why she left?

My head was whirling with thoughts by the time I got to the pub. I saw a tall man with smart shoes, black jeans, a dark-blue shirt tucked in, with a waistcoat hanging over the shirt. He had a really kind face and a very welcoming smile.

He came over to me, held out his hand, and said, 'Hi, I'm Tom,' in a warm farmer's accent that didn't fit his appearance but was soft and made me feel at ease. My first impression was that there was something very likeable about him.

He got me a drink and we sat on a bench outside in the sunshine. He asked if I was OK, as he shifted around nervously. He told me he wasn't sure if I would turn up and that he was glad that I did.

He decided to go in all guns blazing and said, 'I'm not going to beat around the bush, what me and your mum did to you was awful and no amount of anything can undo that. You were three, for goodness sake, but we were both young and naïve. We were in our 20s, and she met me when she was with your dad. She just wanted a fresh start, away from him. She wanted to be with me. She wanted to bring you with her, but she knew if she did that then she would never be free of your dad. I know we were selfish people back then, but we were kids ourselves,' he carried on. 'Your dad said the only way she could leave was if she went to court and gave him full custody of you. So that's what she did. If she could have taken you with us, hassle-free, she would have done, but your dad was a horrible man. He used to hit her a lot, and she wanted to get as far away from him as she possibly could, you understand that, don't you?' He looked at me, but my tears couldn't stop falling. 'Where is your dad now?'

'Prison.'

'Why?'

I told him, but I didn't go into detail.

He then started to cry and blamed himself, out loud. He said that if he hadn't done this or that, things would have been different for me.

He took my hand while he was still crying and said, 'I'm so sorry, from the heart, sorry. If I could go back and do things differently, I would, hand on heart. If I had known the repercussions of my actions back then, I would never have done them. I would have found a different way.'

His sincerity took a load off me. The fact that someone had apologised and owned up to wrong-doing made the whole situation a little bit easier. It was just a shame it hadn't been her.

I asked him to tell me more.

'When you left, none of the family mentioned you ever again. It was like one day you were there, and then the next you were not. Alice's mother removed all the toys, photos, everything on the day of the court case, so it was like you never existed. No one was allowed ever to say your name or make reference to you after that.'

I felt really sad when he said this. It was like I was being erased; who would want to erase a child?

'It was bad for a while,' he said, 'but we all had to do it. Alice cried and said she missed you when it was just me and her alone. She wanted to know you were OK, but couldn't risk going anywhere near your dad, so we moved away. A few months later, we got married, and four years later, we had Sophie.'

There, he said it: Sophie. My replacement. A knife twisted in my stomach, burying itself inside me.

He carried on talking, but all I could see was visions of them playing happy families, them pushing Sophie on a swing, helping her ride a bike, putting a plaster on her scraped knee, reading her a bedtime story, running on the grass with her, kicking the autumn leaves, him carrying her on his shoulders, and Alice holding Sophie's little hand so she felt safe.

I felt a little bit queasy. My stomach churned over and over. I tried to stop thinking and come back into the conversation. I took a mouthful of my drink. He was still talking away about Sophie. He took his wallet from his back pocket and showed me a picture of a pretty 13-year-old girl with curly, brown hair.

I studied the picture. She looked nothing like me. I don't know what I expected her to look like – I didn't really think about it – but she looked happy, really happy.

I felt a lump forming in my throat, so I coughed a little bit and decided to change the subject.

'Was Alice always sick?'

'No, only the past two years. It's been so hard for me and Sophie, watching her deteriorate like that. She was fine and then it got worse and worse, to the point where we didn't have a choice. Things got really bad so we had to put her in the nursing home; we couldn't give her the help or care she needed. That's why I asked the doctor to contact you, because he didn't think it was fair for her to die and for you to never meet her.'

I nodded and asked whether Sophie had a good childhood, and if she was a nice girl. Tom swelled with happiness and said, 'She is amazing, she had the best upbringing, the best that Alice and I could give her. She was always happy and never wanted for anything. She is a good kid.'

My heart dropped to the pit of my stomach. She had the life I always wanted, the life I should have had. I hated myself for feeling this way but I couldn't help it, I felt like I had been robbed, like someone stole my life.

By now, it was really dark; he must have been talking for hours. I slowly got to my feet and told him I thought it was time I went home. He agreed and said, 'Wow, look at the time.'

I said goodbye and he gave me a massive hug and said, 'You take care of yourself. You have to meet Sophie; she would love to see you. I have told her about you and she is really excited about having a sister.'

I smiled weakly and headed for the taxi rank.

In the taxi on the way home, I didn't want to think any more, I was done with thinking for now. I just wanted to rest, so much information, so much to process.

Finding out that Tom was also at fault for Alice abandoning me, and that after I was gone, everyone had to forget me, was tough. And now I knew that Dad was violent to Alice too. And that she got remarried so quickly after she left me, then she went on to have another daughter, who was happy and who got the parenting I should have had. And that Alice wasn't always sick, only in the past two years.

I got home and lay on my bed, emotionally exhausted. Some questions had finally been answered, but I had new information as well. It was all was a bit much for one day. I rolled on my side, curled up in a ball and cried myself to sleep.

CHAPTER TWENTY-SEVEN
On my Own

Age 17

Barbara shouted up the stairs one morning that someone had come to see me and I should get downstairs.

I went downstairs and there was a lady sitting on the sofa. I stood in the room, just looking at her. Barbara gave me a push and said, 'Sit down then.'

I sat down and the lady started to talk. She told me that she was a social worker and that we needed to have a little chat.

Barbara came in and sat in her chair. The social worker carried on talking and said Barbara was tired and needed a break; she'd had a lot on her plate for the last few years and was close to a mental breakdown. So, it was time for me to move out and that maybe space would do us some good.

Barbara butted in and said that I would be fine because I was a fighter and I had always been a fighter.

I didn't understand. *Move out?* Where was I going to go, how would I survive? Everything was still so raw from what had happened, I felt like I couldn't do this.

I had been raped by my father and met my dying mother, and now Barbara was sticking the boot in for good measure.

The social worker said that it was in everyone's best interest and that she had found me a place to live. I needed to get some things together and she would be back later.

I went upstairs and looked at what I had: a few books, my radio, my teddy, my toothbrush and my clothes. Barbara was standing behind me. I turned and told her the things I was taking. She told me I couldn't take the radio as it was originally hers and she wanted it back.

I had so many memories with the radio; so many nights, songs had played while I cried myself to sleep. Other times, songs had played and made me feel slightly happier when the bad stuff was happening.

She gave me a large zip-up bag to put my things in. She looked at me and said, 'I've never had a break. For as long as I can remember, it was always you and your dad, never any time for me. I deserve a break.' Then, she started to cry. 'After everything that's happened, I deserve some me time, and you need to be independent. You'll survive, you always do. It's like it's inbuilt in you. The problem is,' she paused, 'you're just a constant reminder of him and I don't want that in this house.'

I turned away from her and heard her go downstairs. I sat on my bed and cried. I didn't want this, I wasn't ready for this. I didn't know how to live on my own, who would show me?

The social worker came back and was waiting at the front door. I thought to myself, nothing I can do can change this; I'm on my own now.

If I had learnt anything by now, it was that once you get on the crazy train, you just have to keep riding it until it stops.

I walked down the stairs, bag in hand. Barbara was sobbing at the front door, no tears though. I got to the bottom, and she looked at me with her sad eyes and said, 'Bye then.'

I stepped out of the front door, not saying a word to her, I walked two steps and the front door closed behind me.

At the end of the path, I looked back at the house. I tried to think of one really happy memory I'd had in that house. I tried to think of laughter and warmth. I couldn't think of one memory. I was upset because I was being abandoned and uprooted again.

The social worker spoke to me as we walked to her car, but I didn't hear any of it. I was lost in my own thoughts of everything that had happened.

We arrived at a rectangular building with three floors and a lot of windows.

The social worker explained that I would live in this hostel because I was homeless.

I didn't understand what she meant because I did have a home – she knew this because she had just taken me from it.

I didn't say this to her, I just followed her lead.

The social worker pushed a buzzer and a lady from reception came to let us in. I stared at the keypad – so many buttons. The lady introduced herself as Karen. She saw me staring at the buzzers and pointed at them, explaining that there was a buzzer for each room and one for reception. I looked at her blankly and just followed them in.

We walked along a corridor and she showed us the living area, the laundry room, and said each floor had its own communal kitchen.

We went to the second floor, where there were a lot of doors with numbers on them on one side and a lot of windows on the other side.

I leant to look out of one of the windows and could see the other half of the building and the social worker's car, and suddenly had the feeling of being too high up, so I pulled back and didn't look anymore. The social worker and the lady were halfway up the corridor, unaware that I had stopped, so I quickened my pace to catch them up. They stopped at an open door and the lady explained that this was the communal kitchen where residents cooked their meals and could sit and eat together if they wanted to.

The next room would be mine. The lady showed me a swipe card and said this was my key. I was to put it in the slot above the handle of my door. I put the card in and the light on the door went green. I pushed the heavy door and went in to the small room.

To my left was a little table with a TV, by the window was a single bed, all made up. The little window had two tiny curtains; in front of that was a large ledge to put things on. To my right was a wardrobe with two cupboard doors next to it, a little counter top and a doorway. I went to see what was through the doorway. It was my own bathroom: toilet, sink with a mirror above, a shower with a shower curtain and a little window. I tried to look through the crack of the open window and could just see cars moving.

The social worker said, 'Can you give us a minute,' and the lady left. 'This is your home now,' she said, as she took my bag and put it on the bed. 'You can get a poster and put it on the wall, buy some flowers; this is your place now, so make it your own.'

She handed me an envelope. 'Here's some money to get you started. If you need anything, talk to the people at the front desk and they will help you.'

I opened the envelope and inside was a money order. I'd never had money before; I wasn't sure what to feel. She explained that I would be getting a little book in the post and that would give me money every Tuesday to help me live. Again, if I had any questions, I could talk to the lady downstairs. She said I should always take my key with me and not lose it; I had to be responsible for myself now.

'I'll let you get settled in,' she said, adding, 'You'll be OK.' Then, she headed out the door.

I sat on the bed. It was springy but extremely firm, not like my old bed, which was soft and cosy. Already, I missed my old bed, my pillows and duvet.

I sat in the silence, only faint outside noise could be heard. The room felt bare and cold. I decided to unpack, which didn't take long as I hardly had any clothes. I hung them in the wardrobe and opened the cupboard doors next to it, stacked my books neatly inside and popped my teddy on top of them. The books and teddy were eaten up by the vast amount of dark space in there. I shut the door and saw on the counter top that I had my own kettle. What would I use it for? I didn't drink tea or coffee. I don't even think I'd ever used one before.

I put my toothbrush in the bathroom and sat on my bed, looking at the room, alone with my thoughts.

I had been kept like a child for so long. Now, I was thrown into the adult world and expected to just get on with it. I hadn't been taught anything, I wasn't prepared. I wasn't excited, just really scared. I didn't know what I was supposed to do so I just sat there.

Eventually, there was noise outside my door; somebody was outside banging all the doors. I could hear them getting closer and closer. A man shouted and banged really hard on my door. The vibration felt like it filled the room and went straight through me. I started to panic as I sat there, but then heard him carry on further away, and then a door bang as he must have entered his own room.

I sat there uneasy, and wondered what to do. I could sit there in fear or I could lie down and go to sleep. I lay down and tried to shut my eyes, but it felt uncomfortable with them shut so I opened them and looked up at the ceiling. What was I going to do? It was all so different.

I looked down at my hands. I still had the envelope. I sat up. I could go and buy something: food, socks, a book, or a new T-shirt. The possibilities were endless.

I decided that's what I was going to do.

I got up and put my key in my pocket and headed for the door. Carefully opening it, I looked left and right, making sure my door-banging neighbour had actually gone. No one was there, it was safe. As I went out, my door slammed shut with a huge bang. It scared me so much, I ran.

I got to a stairwell and remembered that we had come up so I went down, turned right and opened a door straight into the laundry room, where someone was doing their washing. A woman shouted, 'Wait your turn,' and slammed the door in my face.

Flustered, I kept walking and ended up on a corridor that looked exactly the same as the one my room was on, with exactly the same coloured doors, in exactly the same order, just with different numbers. I felt like I was lost in a maze. A woman came out of one of the doors, steaming drunk, staggered over to me and asked if I had any money she could have. I said no, holding the envelope tighter. She shouted abuse at me and started waving her arms around, so I ran back the way I came.

As I ran back, I remembered the laundry room, and didn't go in this time. Then, I saw the living room and another door, which led into reception.

I went up to the glass window and said I wanted to go and buy stuff, holding up my envelope for her to see. The woman in reception said that town was just the other side of the car park. She said 'When you want to come back in, you hold your key over the sensor till it goes green then the door will open.'

I said, 'OK,' and off I went.

Walking through the car park was quite exhilarating. I had never before been on my own with money and able to buy what I wanted.

I found my way through the car park and was instantly at a shop on the other side. I recognised the town centre from when Barbara and I used to come shopping; now I was just walking distance from it. It was its normally bustly self, with people going in and out of shops, noisy children, and barking dogs. I stood for a moment to take it all in. I was about to join this, I was about to become part of the bustle.

I went into a shop and just walked around, looking at everything, still in awe. I could buy whatever I wanted. That's right, I kept telling myself, *whatever you want*.

I picked up some toothpaste because that was the aisle I hit first and then onto the soap. I had to sniff them all first. They all smelt so different and had different colours. I picked the one that smelt the best.

I carried on walking and saw the food aisle. I was so hungry; I couldn't remember the last time I ate. I grabbed a pack of Jaffa Cakes, a bottle of Pepsi, a multi-pack of crisps and three cans of baked beans. I saw a box of mashed potato; 'just add hot water' it said on the front – it seemed doable for me so I grabbed that too.

Around the corner, I saw a lovely fleecy throw blanket. It looked so inviting, all laid out on the bed. I put all my items on the floor and went to touch it, it felt amazing. I stroked it, it was so soft and fluffy, so inviting that I felt fuzzy with happiness. I wanted it, I needed it, I loved it.

I took the fleece off the bed, picked up all my bits from the floor and put them in the middle of the fleece, then tried to lift it to take it away, but it was just as big as me and awkward to carry. A man in a white shirt and tie came running over and asked if he could help me.

I said, 'Yes, can you help me carry this to pay?' He explained that I couldn't have that one because it was for display but if I waited there for just one minute, he would get me one that wasn't on display.

A few minutes later, he came back with the same fleece but it was all neatly wrapped up with pretty ties around it. I liked this man; he was in the know.

I asked if my other things were display items but he said, 'No', as we unpacked them from the display fleece.

He asked a colleague walking past if they could get him a basket and asked me if there was anything else I needed.

I thought about my room at the hostel and how I didn't have a radio anymore, and how I would miss watching videos, so I said a video player. I loved my videos – they had been left at Barbara's house – *The BFG*, *Benji*, *Labyrinth*. The memory of watching them made my heart flutter.

The colleague came back with a basket and put my items in. The man in the know then took me over to the video player section and asked me what I needed it to do. I said, 'Play videos.' He asked if I knew anything about video players. I said 'No,' so he gave me a video player in a box and told me it was a basic version, as I probably didn't need it to do much. I thanked him, as I didn't need any more help.

I walked to the tills. I had a video player and a fleece in my basket. I couldn't believe it, my own video player and fleece. At the checkout, I put my things on the conveyor belt, the lady scanned them and told me the total. I handed over the crumpled envelope I was still holding. The cashier took out the money order, looked at it, then looked at me. She said, 'I can't take this. You have to cash it first.'

My whole world came crashing down. *I had to what?* I didn't know what she meant.

'Isn't it cash?' I said to her. 'That is cash; the lady told me herself when she gave it to me.'

'I know it's money, but I can't take it like this, you have to get it changed.'

'I can't change it, I don't know where she is to give it back to her to change. I don't know where the lady that gave it to me has gone.'

I started to cry, I had no idea what she was talking about. The social worker told me it was money and now this woman told me I had to change it.

The cashier rang the desk bell and shouted for someone to get the manager. The same man in the white shirt and smart tie who had helped me with the fleece came over and asked what the problem was. The cashier showed him the money order and looked at me.

'Where did you get this from?'

'A social worker lady.'

'Do you know what it is?'

'Money.'

'Do you know what to do with it?'

'Pay for things.'

People had formed a queue behind me and so he took me to one side so they could be served. He explained that I had to take the money order to the post office to be cashed, then they would give me actual money and I could come back and pay for the items. He handed me a tissue to wipe my eyes, and said he would put my basket in a safe place until I came back. He told me where the post office was and that if I got lost, to ask someone. I knew what it looked like because I had been there before with Barbara, I just wasn't sure how to get there from this shop.

So, off I went. It wasn't too far and I felt really lost but I got there after a few wrong turns.

I stood in a queue and waited my turn, took out my money order and handed it over. The man stamped it, stamped something else and then counted out the money really fast. He looked at me and asked if I needed anything else. I shook my head and he shouted, 'Next.'

There was so much money; I was fumbling, trying to pick it all up. It was more money than I had ever seen in my life; it felt like millions in my hands. I was rich.

I stood in the corner of the post office, deciding where to put it all. I still had the envelope from the money order so I stood next to a ledge, turned my back and put all the notes in the envelope one at a time. I put the envelope in the top of my jeans waistband and hid it under my T-shirt, then walked out, hugging my tummy to keep it safe.

When I got back to the shop, my basket was waiting for me and the manager asked if I needed help with anything else.

I said, 'Yes,' and whispered to him that I needed a really big bag for all my money. He showed me the bag section and I picked a small black rucksack.

When I got back to the hostel with all my stuff, I locked my door, put the bags on the floor, drew the curtains and ripped off the ties of the fleece. I lay it on the bed and wrapped myself in it. This was the happiest I had ever been in my life. With the fuzzy, fluffy fleece tucked under my chin, I happily went to sleep where I was.

The next morning, I felt more positive. Positive wasn't something I was used to feeling.

I threw back the fleece and sat up. I was still in the same clothes from the day before, and the things I had bought yesterday, minus the fleece, were still on the floor where I'd left them.

I jumped up and decided a shower and videos were on the list today. I went into the bathroom, no towel. OK, videos and a towel were on the list today. I touched my stomach, the envelope was still there, stuck stiff to me where it had been all night. I checked my pocket, yes, the key was still there. I looked in the carrier bag on the floor, grabbed the toothpaste and speed-cleaned my teeth.

The excitement of what lay ahead today was thrilling.

I grabbed my rucksack, put my envelope with the money in it and headed out the door.

I went to the same shop as the day before and found the towel section; who knew there were so many different colours – big ones, medium ones, little ones, even a pyramid of towels with a ribbon around them. I guessed they were for posh people.

I grabbed a big blue one, strode up to the checkout and proudly handed over my money, smiling, I knew what I was doing this time.

Then, on to the video shop, which was the most amazing place I had ever seen. I loved films. I loved the fact you could watch someone else's story and forget about your own. I had walked past it with Barbara but had never actually been in the shop before.

Standing there, seeing the vast amount of choice before me, all the covers with their different colours and stories, I felt star-struck. I was in my element.

I walked around, familiarising myself with everything, grabbing the films I knew I wanted to watch.

Hours later, I stood at the till with at least 15 films. The man scanned them and I paid, putting some in my rucksack and some in a carrier bag. I walked out, so proud and happy. I was making my life with all the things I loved.

My stomach rumbled so I stopped at a takeaway and got chips, and sat on a wall to eat them. The satisfaction of doing things for myself was amazing.

The chips were so nice, soft, fresh and hot, just what I needed. Afterwards, I headed home. I stopped to look in a shop window. An assistant came to the door and asked if I wanted to look at the mobile phone range they had to offer.

Mobile phones were a new thing. I didn't know much about them, apart from you could call people when you weren't at home, and who would I call? I only had

Emma's phone number so I shook my head and carried on walking.

Just then, I thought about Emma. Where was my favourite book? Emma's phone number was in it. It had gone. Maybe it was at Barbara's house, or had someone to do with the court case taken it? How would I call Emma? I missed her, I missed our chats, I missed having a friend. I missed MY friend. It had been so long since I had spoken to her and so much had happened. I tried thinking of a way to contact her on the walk home, but my thoughts only led me to a dead end. There was no way of contacting her, so I guessed that was that.

I got back to my room and put the videos on the floor, and put the things away from the day before. For a couple of hours, I read and set up my video player while eating Jaffa Cakes.

I took one of the videos from its case and put it on. It roared into play. I jumped onto my bed in excitement and wrapped the fleece around me. I watched intently, soaking up every second of it. Life, at that moment, was good; life was finally how it was supposed to be.

I stayed like that for a week, seeing other people's lives on the screen, all the laughter, the way they lived, the magical feeling that sucked you in. It made me feel content.

That same week, I had learnt that if I followed the instructions on the instant mash packet – boil the kettle, put the mash in a bowl (not the whole box), add boiling water and mix until all powder had dissolved – then I had made mashed potato.

I came up with my own idea of adding cold baked beans straight from the can and mixing it all together. The heat from the mash would warm the beans and voilà, a meal.

That was my dinner every day, and sometimes breakfast. In my little bubble of knowledge, I had learned how to cook and I didn't know what all the fuss was about. It was easier than people made out.

FAX

Social Services
Department

COUNTY COUNCIL

To:		From:	
Phone:		Phone:	
Fax:		Fax:	

Copies:		Date:	*14/9/00*

Number of pages including cover sheet	

Dear ▇▇▇,

Please can you deal with this referral as a matter of urgency, Mrs ▇▇▇ is unable to care for **Child** anymore, and the only other suitable place for her is ▇▇▇ house. The placement is needed as soon as possible

Yours
Sincerly
▇▇▇

P.S If you require any further information then do not hesitate to contact me.

WHAT NOBODY KNEW

This problem affects child herself, as she is very distressed about not knowing where she is going. She has made it dear that she does not wish to remain here in St. Albans. Her stepmother has stated that child becomes more depressed in the house because of the memories. As well as child her stepmother Mrs finds it, very difficult to deal with child's problems and the tension between the 2 is rising to the point where Family members have said that they need separating before one of the does harm to the other child still blames her stepmother for her rape so this causes a lot of emotion within the home and she also receives cards from her dad which is upsetting to her.

At the moment child is staying with her stepmother in the house together and this is a very stressful and unhappy place for child. Her stepmother and her do not get along and her mother has said that if child stays down here then one of them is going to kill the other. I am concerned that child will do herself or the people near her some harm because she is upset and confused about her future

CHAPTER TWENTY-EIGHT
Alice's Funeral

Age 17

Alice died a year after I met her. I was told on the phone.

I hauled myself back to bed, pulled the covers over my head and cried. I didn't cry because she died because I didn't know her. I cried because I was sad how it ended and it hadn't really begun.

It was still painful because I felt like that little girl lost again, who just wanted her mummy, but this time, Mummy wasn't ever coming back.

I pulled my knees up closer to my chest and wrapped my arms around them, letting my sore eyes cry and my broken heart bleed out into my body.

The emotional rollercoaster of disappointment, betrayal, neglect and now death stayed with me for the next couple of days.

If only you could put batteries in people, push their reset button, power them up and hope this time, they would be different.

For me, the physical separation was a burden in itself, but the emotional separation was unbearable. I don't think it's natural for mothers to leave their children, a child they have carried inside them all that time. Imagining what their baby will turn out like, the bond from the very beginning, those first steps you witnessed, those sleepless nights. After three years, you can't just change your mind.

I decided to go to her funeral. I felt it was the right thing to do.

I got given directions by Tom. He said he would be very happy if I would join them and that he hoped to see me there.

My head was still swimming when I arrived. People were pointing and whispering, and I knew it was about me.

Suddenly, it felt like a bad decision, so I decided to go home.

What was I thinking? I didn't know all these people, but they all knew about me.

As I turned to leave, Tom was behind me and put his hand gently on my shoulder and said, 'You came. Thank you for coming, it means a lot.' Beside him was a girl, it was Sophie. There she was, right in front of me, the child that Alice wanted, the child that she chose to keep. I looked at her awkwardly. She seemed very shy but had a kind smile like Tom's.

He introduced us. She said 'Hi' in a sweet and gentle way.

We went in and sat down and the service began. There was a large photo of Alice smiling, which had been put in a frame so she could proudly smile out at the world. I sat down and just looked at the photo. All I was looking at was a complete stranger.

Songs were played, people spoke. I wasn't really listening; I was looking behind me and to the side, just looking at all the people who knew Alice. After the terrible thing I thought she had done, she still had lots of friends and family who loved and cared for her, and had come to pay their respects.

The pastor spoke about Alice, about her life, who she was, and how she was married and had one daughter who she loved very much, Sophie. He went on about her likes and dislikes. People half-heartedly laughed as they remembered the things he said about her life.

All the time, I sat there, feeling like my insides were ready to explode with anger. I replay the words the pastor said: 'One daughter', 'One daughter'.

It's like I never existed. There I was, paying my respects, and I did not even get recognition now that she was dead. Inside, I was fuming.

It was a relief when the funeral was over. I hated what had just happened and was trying to hold the anger in.

Everyone was teary-eyed and huddled together, comforting each other as sad, melodic music played as they all walked out. When I got outside, I started to look for the nearest, quietest corner away from everyone.

I found a bench under a tree, took the cigarettes from my pocket and lit one, taking a deep drag, the smoke hitting the back of my throat, savouring it in a moment of instant satisfaction then blowing the smoke out. That was just what I needed. I needed to calm myself after what I had just heard. Don't make a scene, I thought, not today of all days, just let it go.

I carried on smoking, swinging my feet while I stared at them, trying to process everything that had just happened.

I looked up as Tom came around the corner with Sophie. 'This is where you have got to. I wondered where you were.'

He sat next to me and lit a cigarette. 'Alice would have liked it that you came,' he said. 'It would have made her very happy. She is probably looking at us all now, saying "Dopey lot, crying over me".' He looked up at the sky. 'She is probably having a party up there right now as we speak.

'Your mum was a crazy girl at times, in a good way,' he said. 'God, I miss her so much, we all do.' He finished his cigarette, put it out on the ground and stepped on it.

Sophie sat next to me and smiled weakly. Tom looked at us and said, 'You two can talk for ten minutes and then we have to go to the pub for the wake.' He looked at me and said, 'I look forward to seeing you there, you know where it is, right?' I nod my head. He gave me a thumbs-up and headed off.

I light another cigarette and look at Sophie.

'So, you are my sister?' Sophie asked.

'I guess so.'

'You didn't know Mum, did you, or did you?'

'No, not really.'

She told me how Alice was amazing, that she always loved and cared, she was funny but a little crazy at times, she would jump on the bed with Sophie like a child, and that she didn't have a care in the world.

She glorified Alice, saying what a wonderful mother she was, an angel in her eyes, and she couldn't have asked for a better mother and that she missed her so much.

I could feel a solid lump forming in the back of my throat, and the burn and sting of the tears that I was trying to hold back.

Sophie carried on talking about how she wished I could have met her while she was well. She said that I would have loved her very much because people always did. She told me that her mum was liked by everyone, she always made people happy and was like a ray of sunshine.

I got up, flicked my cigarette and walked away without looking back.

I went home and never went back there.

We clearly had very different viewpoints on Alice, and I had no interest in learning who she was via someone else. I should have had that time with her but she didn't want to be part of my life.

I couldn't play pretend with someone who loved her so much and idolised her, not with my angry, jealous hatred for Alice. It wasn't Sophie's fault, and it wasn't my fault. I couldn't put this behind me and move on, it was too raw.

I could never see her how Sophie saw her or agree with it or listen to how amazing she was.

Every time I replayed what Sophie had said about her in my head, it made me feel sick to the pit of my stomach over and over, making me powerless to control my emotions.

I knew we had the same mother, but we were two different people who were never going to see things the same way. We would never both love Alice the same way.

I was too damaged to ever see things her way, so this was for the best.

When I got home, I sat and cried for days. Everything around me felt dark and lonely again.

Inside, I felt like my body was imploding. I was at breaking point, not sure how much more of this life business I could take.

Everything I had imagined would never come true, everything I had been given was a mess. I had all this information about who I was and who my mother was, and couldn't do anything with it.

But I didn't know who I was. I felt cheated, I felt abandoned for a second time.

I felt like my fantasy of who she was so much easier to deal with than what I had just seen.

My stomach dropped.

I felt like I was still motherless, still childlike, but now more damaged than I was before.

And still alone.

QBDAA 346116

Application Number 7791894/1

CERTIFIED COPY  OF AN ENTRY

DEATH	Entry No. 45

8.   Cause of death
     I(a) Unidentified Leukodystrophy of Brain.

Certified by ▮▮▮▮ MBBS.

"The **leukodystrophies** make up a group of rare genetic disorders that affect the central nervous system by disrupting the growth or maintenance of the myelin sheath, which insulates nerve cells. These disorders are progressive, **meaning** that they tend to worsen throughout the life of the patient."

CHAPTER TWENTY-NINE
Life Skills

Age 17

After my time in my room getting my head together, I decided I needed to leave the room and do something constructive or my thoughts would drive me over the edge. My face had had enough of crying. So, I decided to wash my clothes.

They were looking sorry for themselves and were a bit smelly. I put my pyjamas on and took all the clothes I had down to the laundry room.

When I got down there, I saw someone putting their clothes in, so I watched them from the doorway to see what I was supposed to do. She pushed a few buttons and turned a large round knob, put some powder in a slot box, and then pushed a square green button. The woman looked at me and said, 'You wanna wash? Come back in an hour.'

I took my clothes back upstairs. The buzzer in my room went off, it had never gone off before, and I stared at it, not sure whether to pick it up or not; maybe it was a mistake. I slowly picked up the receiver hanging on my wall. 'Hello,' I said quietly.

A loud voice said, 'Hi, can you come to the front desk please? You have post.'

'OK,' I said, and put the receiver down. I trotted downstairs, and the lady at reception handed me a thick envelope. I opened it and inside was a rectangular, paper printed book. The lady told me it was a benefit book and that every Tuesday, I was to take it to the post office and they would stamp it and give me money. She showed me the pages and explained what everything meant, warning me not to lose it and definitely not to give it to anyone else.

As I walked back, I peered into the laundry room, it was free. I ran up the stairs, two at a time, threw open the door, grabbed my pile of clothes and went down to the laundry room.

I stood in front of the massive drum. I'd never seen a washing machine this size. I tried to see how to open it; I pulled at the door, pushed buttons, banged it, until I saw a scoop in the door like a handle. I put my hand on it and pulled hard. The door flew open and knocked me against the wall. Shocked, I bent down, picked up my clothes and threw them in and shut the door. I looked around, saying, 'Washing powder, washing powder' to myself. There was no washing powder. So, I thought maybe the other lady was using some kind of special powder and maybe the regular washing powder was already in the machine. I stared at the machine. There were so many buttons, there must have been at least 20, and a large, black knob that turned. I tried to see what they all meant but some had symbols and some had words. I couldn't tell what they meant. I tried to remember what the previous woman had done, so I pushed a couple of buttons and turned the big, black knob. I pushed the start button; I knew what that one meant. Nothing happened. I pushed the start button again and again, nothing.

I went to reception and said, 'The washing machine isn't working.'

The lady said that I had to give her money and she would give me tokens. She slid a small, yellow, plastic coin across to me, and said, 'First one's on me,' and smiled.

Back in the laundry room, I looked for a slot, found it, put the token in and the green start button illuminated. I pushed it and the machine started.

I did it. I had washed my clothes for the first time. I stood there and laughed. I had actually done what everyone else in the world did, and I had done it on my own. I ran upstairs and proudly walked along the corridor. I wanted to scream out the window, 'I washed my clothes, world.' But I didn't.

I was excited. I was doing things, and it was mind-blowing.

I made my mash/bean lunch and watched a bit of a film, then went to get my washing.

I opened the big machine door and a whoosh of hot air hit me in the face. I looked inside the massive drum. Something was off. My washing wasn't the same as when it went in. All my clothes had holes in them like big burns, and they seemed smaller. I held them up, wondering what I did wrong. I carried them upstairs all puzzled and unsure what to do. I couldn't wear a T-shirt with a big hole in it.

In my room, I put the clothes on the counter-top and stared at them, trying to work it out. They were ruined and I had nothing left to wear.

Out of the corner of my eye, I saw my rucksack. I didn't feel disheartened anymore, I would buy new clothes.

The only clothes I had left were the ones I was wearing, my pyjamas.

So, I put my rucksack on and headed to town. On the way, I put the old clothes in a bin downstairs.

I got to a clothes shop, which had lots and lots of different styles and colours, and played upbeat music throughout the shop. It was hard to decide where to start.

A pair of blue and white swirly jeans caught my eye first. I grabbed them, a multi-pack of knickers and some socks, picked up three T-shirts and another pair of blue jeans.

I took the jeans to the fitting room and tried them on, I really liked them but they were too big. The fitting room attendant asked me if I wanted help. She asked what size I was and I said I didn't know. I had never bought clothes for myself before, and I couldn't even remember the last time I had had new clothes. She said she had a rough idea and would bring back two different sizes.

I stood there in my PJs, waiting for her to come back.

She brought the jeans and I tried them on, they fitted perfectly. A little giddy feeling of happiness hit me as I stood there, looking in the mirror.

The assistant asked if I wanted to have my feet measured for shoes. I looked at my shoes. I'd had them for a really long time, they were my only pair, and they did look very tired. They were black and the laces were tiny stubs of lace, so not worth being in there. The shoe part had all worn down and bits were hanging off. The rubber at the front had completely come away; I don't know how it still stayed on.

She measured my feet, told me a number and showed me the shoes I could choose. I picked a nice pair of trainers that I really liked the look of.

I loved that I had new clothes. A lot of the time, I'd had second-hand clothes and shoes, and only twice remember getting new clothes when I was younger.

As I stood at the checkout, the women were talking about the rain coming down outside. I looked for an umbrella but couldn't see one. There were lots of hats though so I picked up two baseball caps and thought they would do.

I paid for my things and asked if I could wear the hat now. The lady took the tags off.

I put the hat on and ran through the rain, wearing my PJs and carrying my bag of new clothes.

I stood for a second and looked up at the sky. The raindrops hit my face one after the other, like their sole purpose was aiming for me. I felt free, I felt alive, I was living my life.

When I got back, I immediately put on my new clothes and trainers. I felt brand new. I was a bit nervous because although I felt brand new, I didn't have the comfort of my old clothes. Also, I didn't know how to be brand new. This new feeling was nice but a bit uncomfortable, something I would get used to over time. I still felt broken, I didn't like people and I didn't understand the world. But I had to learn to be brand new.

Trying to be brand new was harder than it might seem.

It had been two years since my dad raped me. You never get over the pain of abuse; you can't run from it, you can't ignore it, and you definitely can't forget it. It's like it's branded into your memory for life, waiting to rear its nasty head at any moment. It makes you feel like you are wired wrong and that you will never be normal.

You see people ambling along, living their day-to-day lives, happy, content, carefree, and you want that, you thrive for it, and feel it's unjust that all that was taken from you.

You are happy some days, then an object, a smell, or something you hear brings all the memories flooding back and you are drowning in a sea of trauma again.

Nobody else can feel it but you, reliving it over and over. Counsellors and therapists don't help; they just make you relive it by talking about it. Any type of reliving it was painful. I was too unstable to talk about it, it made me aggressive.

So, over time, with maturity and distraction, you learn not to heal yourself but to be able to mask it in a desperate need for normality. TV, reading, shopping trips, etc. are distractions that give you a sense of normality, a break from the memories.

But then, someone who looks like him, or a shiny, new belt buckle catches your eye, or you come across the soul-crushing, distinctive smell of John Smith's beer, or you hear familiar songs or phrases. You pray not to remember these things because if you do, the sudden fear makes your heart beat so hard, you feel like everyone around you can feel it beating, one rapid beat after the other. Your brain wants to explode from the sheer panic because you know the memories are coming and there is nothing you can do to stop them; the only option is to run.

But the problem is you can't run from yourself.

CHAPTER THIRTY
Self-Destruct

Age 17

The next few months were a massive learning curve.

My room was getting a more of a lived-in look, and was no longer the empty shell it once was.

When I first moved in, I didn't have time to think of my past problems because learning about the world kept me on my toes. The memories were still there, but pushed away with the need to learn new things.

The nightmares still came every night like clockwork, but as time went on, the demons pushed their way in during the day as well. I started to get submerged in the memories and it was hard to shift them.

A couple of people had said 'hi' in the hostel and had invited me to one of the rooms for a party later that day. I didn't feel uneasy with them asking me, as they seemed quite friendly, and they said a few of the people from the hostel were going.

I was pleased to be asked but didn't feel like going to go to the party; I was happy on my own and I decided I would watch a film instead. But I could hear the music from my room, the booming bass ricocheting off the ceiling and my walls. There was no getting away from the noise.

I turned my TV up as loud as it would go, but the bass from upstairs drowned it out. Against my better judgement, I thought it wouldn't hurt to go along for five minutes to say hi. It was either that or go out. I looked outside and it was hammering it down with rain. That was that decided then. *Damn you, weather!*

The party was on the top floor so I headed up. The room was filled with quite a few people and lots of smoke, the music was really loud, and people were dotted all around, chatting and dancing. This had been the first party I had ever been to.

The noise of people and music seemed to merge into one.

I got warmly welcomed in and someone offered me a beer in a bottle. I accepted it. Laid out on the table were Rizla papers, beer bottles and white powder, which a girl walked over to and hoovered up with her nose.

I didn't like people much, I normally wasn't social, but I tried my best to blend in. By blend in, I mean awkwardly stand by myself, watching everyone enjoying themselves, while holding a drink.

I made my way to an empty sofa. I thought if I sat there, I would look more like I was meant to be there.

A woman with purple dreadlocks and a lip ring parked herself next to me, and introduced herself as Stars. I didn't question her name. She reeled off a bit about herself, asking questions about me along the way, which I didn't answer.

She said to me, 'You don't talk much, do you?' and then went on to tell me who everyone at the party was and their background. I just sat and listened while I watched people dance. I thought I would only stay for a few minutes then just leave. I don't know anyone, and I only came to say hi. The woman spoke very hastily and at any given opportunity, would put her fist in the air and be at one with the beat of the music, swaying or rocking forward.

She sat really close to me and leant into me to speak. She told me she had been divorced and that when she was married, she'd had everything she could ever have wanted; the big house, the nice things, the expensive clothes, and a couple of cars. She had what she thought was happiness for life.

She went on to say she caught him cheating on her and so she left him. She shouldn't have given him such an easy divorce, she should have fought for what was hers, she should have fought for some of the money. She said she didn't because she was heartbroken and wasn't thinking straight, and now she was left with nothing. She said she hated him and hated all men from then on. She said people are shitty and do shitty things, and no one is to be trusted.

I could sort of agree with her on that one, but I didn't make that known.

She said, 'All is not lost though, I've found something magical that takes all the pain away.'

By now, I thought she was sort of crazy, but also intriguing. I looked through the people to find a clear pathway to the door, but I never made it out of my seat.

I don't know why, maybe the intrigue was stronger than the crazy, maybe I could relate to her in some way – we had both been scorned.

She tapped my shoulder and I looked at her. She had green eyes that were so intense, it felt like they looked straight through you. They reminded me of the snake's eyes in *The Jungle Book* that hypnotised Mowgli. It felt like if I stared too long, I would be sucked in.

She tilted her head to one side and said, 'Have you ever had shit in your life?'

I nodded.

She reached into her pocket and pulled out a tiny, clear bag and said, 'This magic pill makes the shit disappear, it makes you forget.'

Inside was a small, thick, white pill with a dove engraved on the top of it. I was really interested by now. I wondered how I had not heard of this magic pill, and why the social worker never mentioned it.

'It's yours if you want it,' said Stars.

'Will I die?'

'No,' she says, 'don't be silly. Why would I give you something that would kill you? You're not scared, are ya?'

As she said that, the hairs on the back of my neck stood up. Dad used to say that phrase to me. Flashes of memories fast-forwarded through my mind.

She took my hand, opened it up and placed the pill in my palm. I looked down at my hand. I could see the lines on my hand wet where I was so nervous. I studied it for a second.

She whispered gently, her lips brushing my ear, 'What are you waiting for?'

I liked the thought of my memories disappearing. I wanted so badly to forget. I wasn't scared anymore, I'd prove it. I opened my mouth and threw the pill back, followed up by my drink.

'That's my girl,' Stars said, and patted me on the back. She shook my hand, smiling, and got up and left, dancing her way through the people.

Half an hour went by and nothing changed. Then, suddenly, I could feel something happening. My insides were gently swirling, my heart beat in tune with the beat of the music. My body and mind were doing something strange and I couldn't stop it. Instinctively, I headed for the door. I thought it best to get back to my room and lock the door.

Back in my room, I felt my jaw stiffen and my teeth clench and start to gently grind. I was smothered in the feel-good sensation, emotional warmth ran full pelt through my veins. I couldn't run from it, and a part of me didn't want to. All I could do was ride it out and enjoy it. It felt so strange but so good. It was like I was on a glorified funfair ride, my mind and body twisting and turning, never knowing which direction was next. I would spin really fast but never get dizzy. My stomach would drop like it did on the Waltzers, then the feeling would rocket back up and make me feel invincible. I was on top of the world, so happy, as the pheromones raced through my body. Ecstasy.

At some point that night, after the buzz had worn off, I had fallen asleep. I woke the next morning and felt ridiculously awful. Lifting my head off the pillow was an effort. My brain felt like it had been repeatedly hit by something hard. I couldn't think properly. My body ached and it felt like my bones and muscles didn't want to work. I tried to think of the previous day and what had happened. I remembered some of it but it was a bit patchy, it hurt to think. My mouth was dry, uncomfortably dry, like I had no saliva left. In the bathroom, I put my mouth under the tap, which felt really good. I drank like I hadn't drank for days. I lifted my head, which really hurt, then I decided to lie down in the hope that maybe sleep could shift this heavy feeling.

I awoke to someone knocking gently on my door, but the way I was feeling, I decided to ignore it. I lay there for a while and then decided to get in the shower. I felt really grubby. I slowly took off my clothes; I couldn't do anything quickly if I tried. I got under the shower and the little drops of water felt like large nails hammering down on my skin. I pulled my shoulders forward to somehow make it hurt less. No amount of scrubbing could make me feel any cleaner; it felt like my skin was hyper sensitive. I showered my face as fast as I could and got out. It helped me to feel slightly better, but not by much.

I attempted to make mash and beans but everything I did felt like it was in slow motion and my hands were shaking. I ate what I could, put a film on and got back into bed. I lay there watching the film but I couldn't register it or process the information properly. I felt there but not there – and not in a good way. My energy levels were zero and it felt impossible to function. So, I slept again.

The next morning I felt loads better, back to my normal self. I thought back over the last two days. The feeling the pill gave me was so amazing, I had never felt anything like it, but the aftermath was horrible.

I was really hungry, so I went out to get some food. I bought my usual mash and beans and stopped at a takeaway to grab chips and some mushy peas. I sat in the takeaway and ate what I could; it felt like my stomach had been an empty void for ages. As soon as I was finished, I picked up my carrier bag and headed home.

As I walked through the main door of the hostel, the woman in reception banged on the glass and called me over. She said I had a letter and I needed to sign for it. Anxious to see who it was from, I signed and instantly knew; the writing gave it away: Emma.

I ran to my room and tore open the envelope, my heart racing in excitement, and there it was, her handwriting.

Emma wrote that she had called at my step-mum's house and Barbara had told her that I wasn't living there anymore and if she wrote a letter, she would post it on to me. She said she missed talking to me and she missed school. She said she hoped I got the letter and to call her or write to her as soon as I could. Her address was neatly written at the top and her phone number at the bottom.

I hugged the letter so tightly and cried my eyes out. She had remembered me. When the world had forgotten about me, she had remembered. She cared, she cared enough to write.

I quickly ran downstairs to the payphone. It read 'INSERT COIN', so I ran back upstairs, opened my rucksack, took out some money and ran back down like the wind was spurring me on. I bolted to reception.

Puffed out, I said, 'Coins for the phone please,' and handed the note over. The lady changed the note and gave me some coins. I kept them all in my hand and put one in the phone, dialled the number on the letter and it started to ring. I was holding onto the phone so tightly, hoping she would pick up.

'Hello?'

'Hello,' I said. 'Is Emma there?'

'Oh hi, love,' her mum said, recognising my voice. 'I'm afraid she's out and won't be back till later. I'm not sure when.'

'Oh.'

My heart sank, I felt like my stomach had dropped to my feet; all the lead up and excitement to be shattered in a second.

'Have you got a number she can call you back on?'

'Erm, no.' I didn't know the payphone number.

Her mum said that she would tell her I called. I said I would call back later and hung up. I was so disappointed that I didn't speak to her, but knew it was really OK because I would call her later.

When I got to my room, I put her letter next to the kettle. I felt alone again. I was so excited to talk to her and she wasn't there.

While my thoughts bounced back and forth, I heard a gentle knock on the door. I got up and opened it. It was Stars from a few nights ago.

'Hello,' she said. 'Mind if I come in? The walls have ears.'

Before I could answer, she had pushed her way in. She sat on the edge of my bed and said she had knocked the day after she saw me but I wasn't in.

'What did you think of the pill?'

I thought about it for a minute, and then said, 'It was good.'

'Good? Is that it? You could at least give me more of an answer than good!' She didn't wait for an extra answer, she just carried on and said, 'Glad you like it coz you owe me £10 for it.'

I said, 'OK,' went over to my rucksack, got the money and gave it to her.

'You liked it, didn't you?' she said, as she held my money up to the ceiling, looked at it and then put it in her bra.

I nodded.

She said, 'There's more where that came from, lots more.' She said she would come by every week with a bagful and I could buy however many I wanted. She said the more I bought, the cheaper they would be. She took out her purse. Inside was a clear bag with 20 or more pills. She held them up, looking at me and said, 'Life is too short to worry about tomorrow; live for today, live for the now.'

I stood there, looking at them, thinking to myself that I did like the feeling the other day, but after the pill wore off, it wasn't so great. But then again, it was not like I had anything to lose. I didn't have memories, nightmares or feel alone when I had the pill.

My thoughts were broken by her urgent question. 'Do you want some or not?'

I panic answer. 'Six. Six.'

I went back over to my rucksack and gave her the money she asked for. She counted the pills out onto my duvet, put the rest away and stood up. She got up and walked towards me, then put her hand on my shoulder and said, 'You and me are mates now, I'll come by next week, see how you're doing.' She opened the door and left.

I quickly locked the door. I picked the pills up and looked at them. They were the same as the one I'd had the other day. I put five of the pills under my pillow for safekeeping and sat on the floor with one in my hand, turning it round and round in my fingers, deciding what to do.

Even though the bad things that happened to me had ended, in my head, they hadn't. I couldn't quiet the monsters within. When I had taken the pill last time, the monsters magically disappeared. The thought of everything that had happened to me up until now ended my hesitation. The pill was gone.

*＊＊

Months went by in a blur and pills had become a constant thing. I'd had speed when pills weren't available and had tried LSD on Christmas Day. I spent my Christmas Day alone: no presents, no tree, just me. Stars had come by and given me a piece of paper that dissolved on my tongue. A little while later, I was tripping.

I sat on my chair and looked down at my legs. From the waist down, my legs had gone so I couldn't get up.

I watched my walls as hundreds of bright red ladybirds went on a mission around the room. I looked over at my door but it was a waterfall. The water was crystal clear and little geckos poked their heads out from behind it, and when they thought it was safe, they would come out and drink.

I lifted my hand to touch my face and my hand was multi-coloured. I looked at my palm and it had three eyes on it, lined up next to each other.

At first, when it started, I was a little bit freaked out, but once I knew I was in no danger, I sat back and enjoyed every minute of it. It was definitely a different experience.

The comedown days made me massively depressed and I felt a desperate need to get happy, like my life depended on it. I was pushing my self-destruct button repeatedly.

Sinking into a wash of drugs, swimming in the high of party central followed by the end of the day, the rock bottom weight of depression.

I had taken my foot off the brake of life and was heading full steam ahead. I didn't want help, I didn't want to talk, it was too late for that.

I started dropping two pills at the same time because one pill didn't feel like enough, and whoosh... my mind would go a million miles an hour, I didn't have time to think. Only feel as the rush snowballed harder, faster.

I'd get an extra sense that you can't explain.

But with double dropping, the comedown would be double doses of depression. A multitude of feelings in a nutshell. Despair. Damaged beyond repair. Being alone. The unknown. Self-destruction. I had become uninterested in anything but where my next buzz/fix came from.

This was my way of dealing with what was, and what had been. Only now, I didn't know how to stop.

Days and nights would blur into one. Alcohol was being thrown into the mix for good measure. On my comedown days, I would wake up and drink instead. One day drugs, one day drink. That way, there would be no comedown.

Then, one day, I didn't have any money for drugs or drink, I had spent it all. I didn't have a single penny and I was having my first proper comedown day in a while.

I sat and looked at my hands; there were blisters all over them, even in between my fingers and on the backs and the fronts of my hands. The blisters had already burst and the outline where they had burst was hard and crusty, with bits of skin hanging off the blister. How had I not noticed that before? They didn't hurt, but my hands looked a complete mess. I could only see a tiny bit of skin on each hand where there wasn't or hadn't been a blister. I thought it must be the drugs.

I lifted my hand to my face. My jaw really ached from constantly grinding my teeth when I was on the pills.

In that moment, I felt like my life was a mess, but this time, I was the one that caused it. I decided enough was enough; it was time to change. I would have to do it all on my own, since I didn't even know how to get help or even how to register for a doctor.

Tuesday came, which meant payday. It had been three days since I had taken drugs and the shakes and the cravings were awful. My sleep pattern wasn't any better either.

I went into town and got my money, and was determined to turn my life around. For the first time in nearly a year, I wanted to spend my money on sensible things. I walked into my favourite place in the whole world, Blockbuster, and went around and around, collecting videos.

I caught sight of myself in one of the mirrors in the shop. I looked so gaunt, my cheeks were non-existent. I was very pale, my skin looked grey, and under my eyes were these huge, dark rings. My T-shirt hung off me because I had become so skinny. I was shocked at how unhealthy I looked. I hardly recognised myself. It made me more determined.

I got my mountain of videos home and vowed to keep the door locked and only leave if I really had to. I was sweating a lot, the craving for drugs made itself known. I would jump up and down to try to shift the feeling, but I was not giving in.

I sat in my room for a week watching videos. The urges had been crazy. I had been vomiting a lot, which made me feel even worse. Some days, I would just lie on the floor next to the toilet because I knew if I moved, I would be sick again. Other days, I would constantly be cold one minute and boiling hot the next.

Stars had knocked a few times but I resisted and didn't answer.

The nights were horrible, the cravings were intense, but I managed to somehow get through it.

Two weeks later, my appetite had slowly come back. My sleep patterns had adjusted, but I still found myself awake in the early hours of the morning.

***

Six weeks on and Stars had stopped knocking. I hadn't touched any drugs or alcohol and I felt a lot better, but hated being me again. The things I had being blocking out came back thick and fast, and made me feel worse than I had originally.

There was a multi-storey car park opposite where I lived. I decided to walk over to it. I stood right at the very top of it, looking up at the birds dancing in the sky; they seemed so happy, happier than me. I thought about what I'd give to go up there and join them.

I looked down; everything was a lot smaller down there. It all looked like miniature toys below me. I walked closer to the edge. *Should I jump?* The feelings of pain would stop if I jumped, the memories would grind to a halt and leave me for good.

It should be an instant death. I would only feel it momentarily, if that.

Then the doubts started. What if I didn't die and just hurt myself really badly? That would defeat what I wanted to achieve.

I shut my eyes and took a deep breath as a welcoming breeze hit my face. I imagined myself falling, the silence was good; it felt right to do this, it felt like it was the only way. I shuffled my feet closer to the edge.

'Only you can do this,' I hear in my head. 'It will free you from everything, being free from the hurt is all you have ever wanted, let yourself go...'

I thought to myself, I decide about my life now, I decide when it ends.

It ends now.

A car horn beeped behind me and startled me. I turned around suddenly. I see two men get out of two cars; they acted like they knew each other, laughing and shaking hands. I looked down and stepped away from the edge. I decided to go home.

As I made my way back down the stone stairwell, the reek of urine bombarded my nostrils. Why do stairwells smell like that, I thought to myself. It was an overwhelming smell of grot. People are disgusting. I hated people. I never asked for the strong smell of urine to be in the same space as me, never have and never will.

As I walked back, I thought about what I had just been about to do. I hadn't been afraid to do it; it had felt like the right thing to do.

The only thing that niggled at me was that if I had done it, I would have felt bad for the person who found me. I felt guilty. Some poor stranger would end up having an awful day because of me and the decision I made.

***

One day, I decided to do a bit of cleaning. I didn't have much so it took no time at all. I leant down to reach for the waste paper bin to empty it and saw some paper behind it. I pulled the bin out and grabbed the paper. Emma's letter; it had fallen down the back of the counter top.

I quickly felt around in my pockets for some money and raced downstairs with the letter, put the money in, dialled the number and waited.

'Hello?' Emma's voice made me so happy.

'Hello,' I said back. 'It's me.'

'I know it's you. Where have you been? Mum said that you called two months ago but didn't leave a number.'

'A lot has been going on.'

'I've missed talking to you; I thought I was never going to talk to you again.'

'Me too,' I said.

'Your step-mum said you're living on your own, is that right?'

'Yeah,' I said.

'Is it OK there?'

I paused. 'It was horrible at first, but I've got used to it now. I had to learn a load of new stuff.'

'Can I come and see you?' Emma asked.

'I don't know,' I replied.

The phone started beeping and I panicked. 'I don't have any more change,' I said. The line went dead. I put the phone down and stared at it. Then I picked up my letter and went to go upstairs.

I put my foot on the bottom tread and I could hear the payphone ringing. I shot back to the phone and hesitated – what if it wasn't Emma? I grabbed the phone.

'Hello?' I said.

Emma said, 'We got cut off. Is it your phone?'

'No, it's a payphone. How did you get the number?'

'I did 1471, silly.'

She said she hadn't spoken to me since before the court case. She spoke very gently and asked if I was OK after all that had happened and that she really hoped I was.

My voice broke as I answered her. I cleared my throat and looked down at my feet, holding the phone tightly and watching my tears race to the floor. There was a small silence.

'Hello?' Emma said softly.

'I'm OK,' I whispered.

'Are you sure?'

'Yeah.'

I was far from OK, but I was better now I was talking to her.

We chatted for what seemed like forever. Emma had a boyfriend and she told me about him, about her mum, her nan, her auntie and her new school. She said at first, she didn't want to go to the new school because she liked our old one and it just wasn't the same. We reminisced about how much we both missed that school.

I told her about what had been going on with me, that I had met my birth mother and she had died, and how lonely I had felt and why I had done the things I had. I told her about the drugs. I also said that I was trying to make myself better and I had lots of videos, which I loved.

Emma said if I wanted, she would write again.

I said I would like that.

When I put the phone down, I didn't feel as lonely any more. It felt good to actually talk to someone other than myself. I was so happy I had spoken to her; it felt like life was worth living again.

CHAPTER THIRTY-ONE
Angel

Age 18

I had been to town, buying my usual bits and bobs; routine was important to me, it stopped me getting trapped in my thoughts. When I came back, there were some residents in the living room, music was playing and it seemed quite relaxed.

My mind thought back to the last time I mingled with the residents and how that turned out. I decided to head to my room. As I was about to walk up the stairs, some guy poked his head outside the living room door and said, 'Hey, wanna shoot some pool?' I knew what that was, I had played it at school and I was pretty good. Because he'd put me on the spot, I agreed, and followed him into the living room where he handed me a pool cue. I played a game and lost. I didn't do too badly, and just put it down to being a bit rusty.

I sat down, people came over to chat and I chatted back. I still didn't understand people, but I didn't feel as shy anymore. It was like the drugs had unleashed something in me, and now that I had been in the hostel for a while, I didn't feel as scared there as I once had.

I sat on the chair and listened to the people laughing and the music playing. In that moment, I felt something, it wasn't home, but it was OK.

A girl I hadn't seen before walked in through the living room doors. All the people in the room, including me, were sitting in a semi-circle, talking. She came over and sat on one of the chairs and joined us.

She said, 'Hi, my name is Angelina, I just moved in downstairs so I thought I would introduce myself.'

People immediately warmed to her and started talking. I got up and sat on an empty seat next to her. I thought she was so brave to introduce herself like that to all these strangers. She was very positive and oozed confidence. I liked her. She spoke nicely and held herself well. She didn't seem at all phased by people the way I was. She spoke to them each in turn and knew exactly what to say at the right time. I would fumble or speak too fast or hesitate, but she didn't seem to mind that about me. We instantly hit it off. I went back to her room because she said she was hungry and could make us something to eat.

She had made a soup from scratch and invited me to eat with her. The soup was made of potato, cabbage, beetroot and carrot. It smelt amazing. As we ate it with some bread, I loved the way the flavours danced around my mouth. She told me she was originally from Russia and was 17, the same as me. As we ate, she told me stories of her time growing up in Russia and that this soup recipe was one she had learnt to make there. I listened intently, asking questions when I didn't understand. I had never been to another country before so it was interesting to learn all about Russia.

I had been living solely on mash and beans for nearly a year. It was great, don't get me wrong, but it was refreshing to try something new.

We finished the soup and bread. I showed her my room and she liked that I loved films. I had the film *Kickboxer*, which she said was one of her all-time favourites, so we sat and watched it together. We sat on my bed, our backs pressed up against the wall, fleece thrown over us, eating Jaffa Cakes while we watched.

It was strangely comforting, watching a film with someone else; I had been so used to watching films on my own. She would talk, laugh and ask me questions about the film. My heart would jump because this brought a new meaning to the film. As two people, we couldn't have been more different, but we were in the same situation and were the same age, which brought us together.

We spent just about every day together after that first meeting. I shortened her name to Angel because I felt it suited her better, and it did. She would come up to my room and watch videos; she even regularly ate my mash and beans! It felt good to have the comfort of someone else to laugh with, it made living on my own less scary because Angel hadn't lived on her own before either.

She believed in living the right way, not hurting people. She didn't drink alcohol, she had never smoked or taken drugs, she didn't swear, and she would never talk about vulgar things. Most of all, she didn't try and be someone she wasn't; she was happy with who she was and where she came from. Whereas, I didn't have a clue who I was and hated where I came from.

Angel would go to college Monday to Friday and I would do my day-to-day things and then wait for her to come back and tell me about her day.

Our friendship grew and grew. We talked about what we would do when we were 30, which seemed a million miles away to us, but we were determined to do so many things before then.

I liked the way she was fun, I liked the way she made me smile. She loved to dance, any kind of music, and she would click her fingers, swing her hips and her arms passionately like she was at one with the music.

My dancing was unexplainable and I hated doing it.

Neither of us could sing a single note in tune, but we sung anyway, together. Loudly and proudly.

One day, Angel said she wanted to explore and suggested that we go to London. Wow, I thought, London. I had heard about it, but had never been. Angel said we should get the train and see where we end up; she said it was an hour away on the train. I felt exhilarated for so many reasons, it was an adventure. Where would we end up? Would we ever come back? I had never been on a train by myself before! We marched to the train station, all chatty and excited about what we were going to do. We got travel cards, which meant we could go anywhere in London, as long as we came back before midnight, when the travel cards ran out.

I felt so grown up, travelling on the train with other grown-up people. I had no idea where I was going, but I wasn't scared because I was with Angel.

I looked at all the people on the train. Some were reading newspapers; others were just aimlessly looking out of the window. What amused me the most was the amount of people asleep.

I said to Angel, 'Should we wake them up because they could end up anywhere?'

Angel looked around at them and whispered that I should mind my own business, they knew what they were doing because they probably did the same thing every day, and they could probably hear me talking about waking them up, and that I was to shh. I agreed, but I still thought it was a good idea.

Angel stood up and studied a map on the carriage, and explained that we should get off the train at Kings Cross and get on another train to Piccadilly. I looked at the map but had no idea how she came to that conclusion. It was just squiggles, names and colours to me.

I loved it when Angel and I were talking and another train rushed past the window. It would give me such a fright; it felt like in that second, my heart had stopped beating. The way it rushed past was like the excitement I felt for our journey. I liked the silence after it had passed and the fact that everything would return to normal.

Angel navigated us all the way to Piccadilly. Whenever we went the wrong way, she would navigate us back. I had no idea how to do this travelling business unless a sign was right in front of my face, yet I watched everyone else do it with ease. They all knew where they were going, bags in hand, weaving in out of people's way to get to where they needed to be.

'Come on, what are you doing?' Angel shouted. I had stopped momentarily to watch the people. I quickly jogged to catch her up, dodging the people along the way. Angel told me that we mustn't lose each other because London was such a big place; we had to stay together at all times.

We got off the tube and the melodic sound of 'please mind the gap' made us smile as we mocked it.

Coming up the steps, I had my head down, listening to Angel talk. When we reached the top, I looked up.

I stood there and stared. The lights, the buildings, the people. It was a whole other world; it was like a childhood I should have had, full of excitement and adventure, with lots of things going on.

For the first time in a long time, I felt a true happiness that wasn't chemically enhanced. I was high on life and I had my friend with me. At that moment, I didn't need anything else.

It had got dark and the lights shone their brightest, like they were lighting up the sky.

In front of me was a gigantic building, completely lit up with advertising signs. It looked so magical in the dark, it kept changing to different logos, and I just stood there in awe, watching it past the bright red double-decker buses, taxis and cars on the road in front of us.

The different smells of food hit me as the wind blew them in my direction. I breathed the aromas deep into my lungs.

'Wow,' Angel said. 'Come on, let's go and have a look.'

We passed a huge fountain with four large statues of horses up on their hind legs, like they were going to jump right out of the water. We stood and looked up at them as they towered above us, their hooves ready to trample our heads if they came alive in that moment. The detail on them was so beautiful.

As we walked on, I was amazed to see shops and restaurants open at night-time; we never had that where we lived, everything shut at 5p.m. They were all so busy.

I kept stopping and looking in shop windows at all the wonders they had to offer. I had never seen anything like this, it really was like a different world to me. Angel linked her arm through mine and said, 'Come on, there is loads to see,' and pulled me along to see something else.

We passed a man selling roses for £3 each. Angel said she only had five pence. The man said, 'OK', handed over the rose, and said, 'A pretty rose for a pretty lady.'

We both laughed; we were dumbfounded at that happening and thought it must have something to do with the magic of London, and that anything was possible here.

We saw a huge arcade, it was enormous, with so many games to play on. The machines all lit up with their music playing at the same time, it drew us in. We had a look around and decided what we would play on next time we came, as neither of us had any money.

Angel had a small camera with her that she used for college. She took pictures of all the things that were new to us.

There was a security guard inside Starbucks, which we thought was really strange. Who would want to steal coffee?

We dared each other to see who was brave enough to take a picture of him, as we wanted to remember that moment. Neither of us were, so we left it and carried on.

We heard some music in the distance. Angel said, 'Can you hear that?' then started to dance. 'We need to find where that music is coming from, come on,' she said. 'Follow me.'

We ran until we came to a circle of people clapping. Angel grabbed my hand as we pushed our way through the crowd to the front.

In the middle of the crowd was a very pretty woman, wearing a bright red flamenco dress. There was a stereo playing what sounded like a Spanish guitar and a man's voice, singing in Spanish. She was dancing very gracefully to the melodic music like she had danced this dance a million times before. Then people started clapping as the music got faster, the dancer flicked her dress, twisting her arms in the air and stamping her feet in shoes that clacked every time her feet hit the floor.

I was laughing so much at Angel, who was trying to imitate her.

The music got a lot faster and every single person was clapping and cheering. The dancer held her dress up slightly and her footwork was fast and precise with the constant clacks of her shoes to the beat of the music. She swayed her dress one way then the other while still doing her steps.

The beat repeated over and over and she spun herself round. The bottom of her dress became a blur so you couldn't see where it started and ended; it spun like a spinning top, round and round as she went faster and faster until the beat ended and she stopped instantly in a dramatic pose.

The crowd of people went crazy, whistling, cheering and clapping. The dancer took a bow several times and went to the side of the crowd to get a drink.

The music started again. Angel was all geared up by this point; it looked like if she couldn't dance, she was going to burst. She pulled me out into the middle where the dancer had been, dancing all the way. I just sort of danced the best I could, which was awful – I had no rhythm and no direction. I was really nervous as it was just the two of us and it felt like the whole world was watching. Angel danced so well, she spun around, mimicking the dance the flamenco lady had done, and was doing her own fancy footwork, the flamenco dancer watching and clapping her on.

Suddenly, other people from the crowd joined us and started to dance. My nerves disappeared. I don't remember how I danced but I just went for it.

All I could hear was laughter and the music, all I could see was Angel and people dancing. Angel grabbed my hand and spun herself under it, smiling. She was loving this. The music got faster. Angel spun. I spun myself and looked up at the night sky. The stars were so bright. I looked back at Angel, who was still spinning. The music stopped and Angel stopped and stood in a dramatic pose. I laughed so hard.

She finished her dramatic pose and laughed with me.

The train journey home was just a buzz of excitement about our new findings and achievements. We were talking so much, we nearly forgot our stop.

We both agreed we would definitely go to London again because there was so much more to explore.

We said our goodnights, and that we would see each other the next day.

Both of us knew that our adventures hadn't finished, they had only just begun.

Chapter Thirty-Two
The Funfair

Age 18

Angel said one day on the way home from college that she had seen a poster for a funfair that was in town and we should go. It would be fun. I liked the way Angel was spontaneous and carefree. I knew she understood dangers and liked to avoid them, that's why I felt so safe with her.

As we were getting ready, she came up with a genius idea. She said we should go and work for the fair.

'It would be amazing,' she said. We would travel the world, watching people on the rides, we would live on the road, and it would be our job, so we would never be short of money. And the most important thing was that we would be able to ride the rides as many times as we wanted. Wow, I thought, she had a point. I had no education since my school closed down, and no one had ever talked to me about getting a job; it sounded exciting. I had no commitments and I remembered the trip to Piccadilly and what a magical place the world was. So, I agreed, as long as I could take my videos with me though, because I couldn't live without them.

Angel frowned and said, 'When are you going to find time to watch videos if we are all over the world, busy working for the fair?'

I told her I would make time, so Angel agreed and said the videos were the only thing I could take round the world with us.

We headed towards the field where the funfair was being held. You could hear it before you could see it; the excitement of the music made us quicken our pace.

There were so many rides: Waltzers, and a huge seated ride that went up in the air and back down again and then to side to side and round in a complete circle really fast. There were children's rides, hook a duck, and a coconut shy.

Most of the rides had bright flashing lights, while blasting out modern, upbeat music.

We both decided that the huge seated ride was the best in the whole fair. We only had enough money for one ride so that was it.

We got on and strapped in. It was only Angel and me on the whole ride, which could fit 18 people.

As the ride rose really high, Angel screamed with delight, with her hands in the air.

I held onto the security brace tightly with both hands. All the different bright, coloured lights flashed simultaneously, the music boomed out, the ride swung us round and round, side to side and up and down. It would slowly swing us one way then violently swing us the other.

Angel shouted to me, 'Put your hands in the air,' but I held on even tighter. Not knowing which way the ride was going to go made me think it was going to throw me out of my seat, and it was a long way down.

Angel shouted, 'It's OK, put your hands up.' The ride slowed slightly so I let go and put my hands in the air – instantly, the ride swung fast round in a circle. Angel screamed, 'See, it's more fun when you let go.' I kept my arms in the air and she was right, it was a lot more fun if you let go.

The ride came to an end; the adrenaline fuelled us along. We were ready for anything.

As we got off, Angel asked the ride attendant if there were any jobs going. He said to go and ask the other man at another ride.

We went over and she asked the same question. He said there was and we could each have a stall right away. I got the hook a duck stall. Each time a child came over, I would ask for the money and then hand them a fishing rod. I let them hook a duck, bobbing around on the water. If they got the right number, they won a prize.

At first, I was so nervous, I thought the children could tell by my eyes that I had no idea what I was doing.

Half an hour or more in and I was getting confident, shouting, 'Roll up, roll up, come and hook a duck and win a prize.' I started to feel like I owned the duck stall and was quite happy for it to be my permanent job for the rest of my life, just like we'd planned.

Lots of people came and went throughout the evening and eventually, it was time to finish. We helped pack away our stalls and others, and helped pack up the rides where we could. Angel got out her camera and someone took a picture of us outside our favourite ride before it got packed away.

We went over to the man who had given us the job and took the stalls' takings and went to give it to him. He said that it was OK, and that we could keep the money, as we'd earned it. It seemed like a lot. We told him we would be back tomorrow for some more work.

All the way home, we were so excited. We were officially funfair workers and we'd got paid. Our lives were changing; we were going to be superstars.

The next day, I waited for Angel to come back from college, itching to go to the fair. She said there wasn't any point in us leaving until 6p.m., so we still had plenty of time to have something to eat and get ready. I had been ready for hours, but Angel got ready and we sat down and ate something.

By the time 6p.m. came and we were about to leave, Angel told me not to seem too eager because they would put us on the silly stalls. She explained we needed to show maturity; that way, they would let us control the bigger rides eventually.

We headed off, skipping excitedly as we went.

When we got there, there was no music, no lights, no rides, just a bare field and turfed-up grass.

We both stared, disappointed and deflated.

Neither of us said a word. Eventually, Angel put her arm around me. She said, 'Don't worry, at least we worked on the fair.' She turned me round and we started to walk home. She carried on. 'Who can say they worked on the funfair and actually got paid for it? It will come back next year and we will be here the first day it sets up, so we can work from day one till it ends.'

'What are we going to do now?' I asked.

'Do you have any mash and beans?'

'Yes.'

'Mash and beans and watch a video then.'

And that's exactly what we did.

CHAPTER THIRTY-THREE
Dad's Death

Age 18

I got a phone call from one of my dad's brothers. I don't know how he got my number but that didn't really matter.

My dad had six brothers. Throughout my whole childhood, they stayed away and we never saw them. I think it's because they knew how destructive Dad was and they didn't want any part of it.

My dad's brother told me he'd been trying to track me down to give me the sad news that Dad had died. He told me that Dad had a heart attack that killed him outright in prison, and it was likely that all the drink and cigarettes had finally taken their toll on him. He said that he would call me back to let me know when the funeral was. He told me that when Dad died, he didn't have a penny to his name, and as I was his next of kin and his only child, the funeral costs fell to me, but that I didn't have to worry about that as he and another brother had already covered the costs. He added, 'I'm very sorry for your loss,' and the phone went dead.

I remember those words because I remember not feeling as if it was a loss.

I cried so hard because it was finally over. I cried tears of relief. I was finally free. He couldn't get to me anymore. He would never touch me again. He couldn't hurt me anymore. I could stop living in fear of him. The nights I would wake up in a sweat, thinking he was in the room, would be no more. I wouldn't need to keep looking over my shoulder just in case he was there. I didn't need to catch my breath in the dark because I thought I heard something. I could be whoever I wanted to be, finally, I could be me. The real me who I was meant to be.

That's why I cried, and the only reason. A massive part of me was devastated that he never apologised for what he had done and not being the father he should have been from the beginning, but then in my heart, I always knew that would never happen.

Later on, my uncle called to tell me which day the funeral was and what time.

I politely declined the invitation.

There was no way I was going to his funeral after everything he had put me through. Funerals are where you pay your respects, and I did not respect him at all. I was glad that he was dead; that way, he couldn't hurt people anymore. He couldn't hurt me.

I believed karma had come and served him justice for all the bad decisions he had made. He was in his 50s when he died. His life got cut short and he only had himself to blame.

A few days after his funeral, the nightmares started again. I had dreams that he was in the same room, that he was raping me again, beating me again, laughing at me. I dreamt of Alice too. She looked the same as when I saw her in the nursing home, but she said, 'I didn't want you, I never wanted you,' over and over. The dreams shook me to my core. I would wake up terrified and feeling awful. I would know it was a nightmare but I couldn't get rid of the feeling it gave me.

At this time, I shot into a whirlwind of drink. It may have been over but I couldn't shake the demons dancing around in my head, the memories constantly in the forefront of my mind, the scars that he had left, the trauma he had caused. The memories I couldn't shake were a day-to-day burden.

I thought to myself: he is gone now and you are finally free. You have hope. But there was a constant reminder when I woke up and looked in the mirror. I had his deep, dark, burning eyes. The circles under my eyes looked just like his when he leaned in close and head-butted me in the face. My dark eyebrows were the same as his; I felt they gave me an added extra look of evil. I stared at myself in the mirror, hoping that one day, I would no longer look like him. But as he told me many times, I was his, I always would be his, and I would never be able to change that.

The drink put me in a different place, a place the memories couldn't reach. It was a temporary fix that lasted a year or more, it was hard to tell. Angel kept her distance; she didn't like me when I was drunk. While I was intoxicated, it blocked out the flashbacks, but at the same time, I lost control of myself. I wanted to go higher and faster, for it to last longer, for as long as the buzz lasted, I wasn't me anymore, I wasn't living my life. In my mind, I was somewhere else, and that on its own was addictive enough.

As the liquid trickled down my throat, the sharp chill conquering its way down to my stomach, the addictive feelings that had badgered me constantly for this rose to the top to bask in the liquidy goodness.

The satisfaction void was never filled completely.

The scariest part was that when I was sober, I would think about all the drink I had consumed the night before. Was I becoming him? I couldn't turn into him. I didn't want to. I would drink more to block out those thoughts.

This was just a coping mechanism. Wasn't it?

Night after night, one drink chased by another, sometimes having two drinks at a time.

I had this stupid idea that the more messed up I could get, the more normal I would feel, because when I was drunk, I didn't care anymore – I felt like I was perfect.

The point came when I didn't know who I was anymore, sober or drunk. Vomiting was the sign I had gone too far. Many friendships had been made and broken. Angel watched on, disappointed at what I had become. I remember being so drunk on the floor and her shouting at me for drinking like this. I cared and I wanted to change, but in that moment, I was powerless and couldn't stop what had begun, not yet anyway.

The drunk me was a wild child who didn't care about anyone or anything. Nothing could hurt her; she had been through hell and back and wanted to prove to the world she wasn't scared anymore.

The rape still haunted me; even though Dad was now dead, the dark memories of those days weren't. I never completely got over it and I'm not sure I ever will.

The alcohol made me brave, bold and loud. The sober me would hate the drunk me and, in a way, was slightly terrified of her. Sober me was desperate to live a normal life and knew drunk me was wrong, yet I would still crave the drink and the lifestyle.

It was like a Jekyll and Hyde situation. There was a constant battle with myself: which way was the right way to go?

The drunk me would always win, because in her head, people had always controlled her, beaten her down and degraded her, and while she was flying high on booze, she was brave enough to be her own boss and take control, and she wasn't going to have anyone control her again.

I don't know if the drinking was a cry for help or whether it was a coping method, but it ran its course and eventually came to a halt.

Because one day, I met him.

CHAPTER THIRTY-FOUR
Write What You Know

He had a confidence about him, a confidence that automatically made you feel safe. He was one of those instantly likeable people and I loved his personality. He didn't shout, was calm and always level-headed. He liked to party but he wasn't an alcoholic. He was well travelled and well spoken. He had done and seen many things and enjoyed the finer things in life.

I met him in a pub. I knew people that he knew and we ended up sitting at the same table on a Friday night. His eyes were his key feature; you didn't want to look away from them when he spoke, because his eyes were not only kind but seductive. There he was, drinking and laughing with me, and he wanted nothing more than friendship.

We met up in a group a few times, Angel came along as well and we went clubbing in London with him. He knew which clubs were the most popular and Angel and I had never been clubbing before so it really opened our eyes. The whole time, he was a gentleman, took us out, got us home safe. We became friends with his friends and so the group of us met up every weekend to go out.

There were many nights when we drank, we talked, we laughed, we drank some more. Then one night, we drank too much, his calming voice whispering in my ear, his gentle touch making me weak at the knees. Then, for the first time in my life, without hesitation, I made love to him. It was the alcohol that gave me the courage to sleep with a man. Without alcohol, I probably would never have done it once in the whole of my life.

Him mixed with the alcohol. In that moment, all the problems that made me who I was disappeared. It was one of the best decisions I have ever made.

It was a whole different life to what I knew; sex like I hadn't known it, love that I hadn't felt before.

The sleepovers happened more and more, the awkwardness afterwards slowly disappeared, and I ended up being at his place more than my own. He kept his house very orderly and everything had its place, which impressed me.

As time went on, he asked me to move in. Nervously, I agreed, and packed my little bit of nothing and took a massive risk. He taught me the skills that my parents should have passed down to me: how to cook, quality over quantity, how to take care of the things you own, how to wash clothes properly.

Him being so normal made me feel grounded. When we were together, I spent my life trying to be normal and trying to fit in, hoping no one would notice how damaged I was.

***

Over time, I told him my story. Each time, he listened attentively. He was very understanding, which must have been difficult for him, considering his background was completely different to mine. I was lucky to find someone who tried to understand all I went through and is always there for me. I love the way he stands by me, regardless of what has happened or what will happen. Over time, we had our ups and downs, the same as all couples. This is where I learnt how to compromise.

I would overthink things and over-analyse situations from every angle. I didn't mean to, it was just my way. It was who I had been made into.

I would have anxiety attacks where I couldn't breathe, then the world would slow right down and then, within a second, spin really fast. My stomach would knot up and my heart would beat uncontrollably fast, my palms laced with sweat, breathing fast in, out, in, out, just trying to keep up with the speed of my body. He would stand there, watching, powerless to help, while I panicked and rode it out.

Eventually, I went to the doctor and got some medication to stop the world spinning. I couldn't pinpoint what the causes of it were, but was glad that it was under control.

CHAPTER THIRTY-FIVE
Me today

When I was 25, I changed my name. I decided to re-invent myself, and become someone else – someone who wasn't damaged, who wasn't a victim. I was going to try and start being me, the me I was supposed to be.

I never wanted children, mainly because I thought I could never be a good mother. I thought I could never protect them from the world. I knew the nasties of the world and what they could do. All the bad things that happened in my life taught me an invaluable lesson: what not to do

However, I took a huge leap and had a child, which was a massive learning curve in itself. So now, I'm being a mother while being motherless, with no one to guide me, but I'm pretty sure I won't make the same mistakes my mother did, and definitely not the ones my dad made.

I'm happy where I am now; I no longer have a reason to be scared.

So many times throughout my life, I could have died, and now, I have an opportunity to live, a reason to live, with someone who wants me to live so he can love me.

I will never completely get over any of what happened, my demons will always stay with me. I just have to learn to deal with it. I have to; otherwise, it will destroy me.

Today, I'm a new me, a happy me.

As my now husband once said, 'I will still love you regardless. Let go of what you know and start your life with me.'

And so, that's exactly what I did.

Lightning Source UK Ltd.
Milton Keynes UK
UKOW04f1058141217
314463UK00001B/7/P